G000153813

The Business of Law

Strategies for Success

Consulting Editor **The International Bar Association**

Consulting editor
The International Bar Association

Publisher
Sian O'Neill

Editor
Carolyn Boyle

Marketing manager
Alan Mowat

Production
Russell Anderson

Publishing directors
Guy Davis, Tony Harriss, Mark Lamb

The Business of Law: Strategies for Success
is published by
Globe Law and Business
Globe Business Publishing Ltd
New Hibernia House
Winchester Walk
London SE1 9AG
United Kingdom
Tel +44 20 7234 0606
Fax +44 20 7234 0808
Web www.globelawandbusiness.com

Printed and bound by CPI Group (UK) Ltd, Croydon, CR0 4YY

ISBN 978-1-905783-61-8

The Business of Law: Strategies for Success
© 2012 Globe Business Publishing Ltd

DISCLAIMER
This publication is intended as a general guide only. The information and opinions which it contains are not intended to be a comprehensive study, nor to provide legal advice, and should not be treated as a substitute for legal advice concerning particular situations. Legal advice should always be sought before taking any action based on the information provided. The publishers bear no responsibility for any errors or omissions contained herein.

MIX
Paper from
responsible sources
FSC® C013604

Table of contents

Preface

Lord David Gold

We are light years away from the time when law firms were prohibited from having more than 20 partners. In the last 30 years we have seen the top solicitors' practices grow both in size and in geographical reach. The City firms have become major businesses and are competing around the world with the best firms from the United States, Australia and Europe. While these firms have recognised that if they are to stay on top, they must continue to provide the very best legal services, as major businesses they have also had to put in place the right structure and management system to enable them to compete and continue to grow.

Law firm partners are not natural business managers and yet traditionally partners have resisted management from non-lawyers. So rather quickly, and with varying degrees of success, law firm leaders have had to learn how to be managers.

Uniquely, this book brings together guidance from a number of experts and skilled practitioners who have crossed over from practice to management and have taken their firms forward most successfully. Those contributing here have a wealth of practical experience to share, including on succeeding within your jurisdiction, the role of governance and corporate social responsibility, developing effective PR strategies and profitability drivers and financing techniques for law firms, among other practical aspects of managing a flourishing legal practice. They have had to deal with many of the issues that confront all law firms as they grow, and I have no doubt that the reader will benefit from their insight.

Lord David Gold is a legal strategist, a mediator and a Conservative working peer. He was also appointed corporate monitor of BAE Systems plc by the US Department of Justice in August 2010. He was formerly head of litigation and then senior partner at Herbert Smith LLP.

Instead of taking the lead in conducting litigation, Lord Gold offers to work alongside the client's existing solicitors to find a solution to the problem as an additional resource to the team. Lord Gold will bring an objective, commercial and fresh view to the problem, including a review of strategy.

Lord Gold has a pre-eminent reputation as litigator and is recognised as one of the country's leading litigators by all of the top legal directories. His clients have included many FTSE 100 and leading international companies, major investment banks and high-profile individuals.

Acknowledgments

The publishers would like to thank the International Bar Association (IBA), and particularly Paul Crick and James Lewis, for suggesting the proposal for this book and for their creativity in revising it to its existing structure. Thanks also to Ed Green and Neil Smith at the IBA for working with us to promote the book.

Particular thanks are also owed to Stephen Denyer, chair of the Law Firm Management Committee of the IBA, for his time and all his invaluable suggestions and contacts. The book, of course, would be nothing without its contributors, so a big thank you to all contributors, including Lord David Gold, for their time and effort in sharing their experiences with us and our readers.

Sian O'Neill
Publisher
Globe Law and Business

Business models and strategies: the current state of the art

Stephen R N Denyer
Allen & Overy LLP

1. Introduction

Lawyers in the past often used to debate whether or a law firm was a 'business' or a 'higher calling' to which business concepts were anathema. Now, in the 21st century, it must surely have become obvious that this debate is over. Although lawyers are not (generally) just in it for the money, law firms must be developed and run on the basis of sound business principles or they will not be successful in today's competitive environment.

One of the key features of any successful organisation (business or otherwise) is a sound strategy. This must be developed through a rigorous process and tested thoroughly against the harsh realities of day-to-day activities. Law firms need strategies more than most. The barriers to entry into the legal services market are so low and the market everywhere is so fragmented that any firm without a strategy will be lost.

The purpose of this chapter is to offer some practical thoughts on how a law firm might develop its strategy. These thoughts are influenced more by my experience as the current chair of the IBA's Law Firm Management Committee than they are by my experience as an Allen & Overy (A&O) partner. Although I have learnt a lot at A&O, it must be said that developing a strategy for a global giant such as this will differ somewhat from the strategic planning process of a smaller and less global organisation. I have attempted to direct my comments towards the latter rather than the former.

2. Getting started

Law firms are run by busy people who generally want to be lawyers rather than businesspeople. For this reason many of them struggle to get properly started in the strategic planning process. In my view, the best way to go about this is to consider the following five issues:

- the firm's existing strengths, weaknesses, opportunities and threats (SWOT);
- the firm's culture and values;
- the firm's preference for evolution or revolution;
- the competitive environment in which the firm operates; and
- the people who should be involved in the process.

2.1 Existing strengths, weaknesses, opportunities and threats

It is impossible to get where you want to go if you do not know from where you are starting. Any law firm's strategy must therefore begin with a rigorous analysis of the situation in which the firm finds itself. In the case of a new firm, this will be the situation in which the founding partners find themselves. Such an analysis is best done through a traditional SWOT analysis, which should be written down and brainstormed by the core group within the firm that will advance the strategic planning process. The way to do this is to consider strengths first (eg, a practice area where the firm is particularly strong), and to set against those weaknesses (eg, a different practice area where the firm is not strong at all). You should then proceed to the opportunities (eg, the chance to upgrade the firm's client base as a result of adding additional practice areas), and set these against threats (eg, new competitors entering the market). All four categories are best placed in a two-by-two box matrix which looks like this:

Strengths	Weaknesses
Opportunities	Threats

In my experience, lawyers tend to be extremely optimistic about their strengths and to underestimate their weaknesses. An effective SWOT process therefore requires a degree of rigour. A good way to do this is to involve actual or potential clients, so that you can compare the insiders' views of the firm with an external perception that derives from a comparison with other firms of a similar kind.

In the case of a newly established firm, as with the SWOT analysis (referred to above), the best way to deal with matters connected with culture and values is for the founding partners to consider what they most valued about their previous firm or firms and to devise a vision for the new firm which is informed by that prior experience.

2.2 Culture and values

Every law firm I have ever dealt with has a culture of some kind. This is always underpinned in a certain way by the values espoused by the firm. It is essential that the firm's strategy be aligned with its culture and values. A firm with a 'consensus' culture is never going to succeed in implementing a strategy involving rapid and radical change. Similarly, a firm whose values rely on operating as a single integrated entity will not feel comfortable with a strategy that involves creating a lot of separate profit centres under a loose overall umbrella.

In determining its culture and values, a firm will do well to encompass a broad range of stakeholders. These should include all those currently within the organisation, not merely the partners and the lawyers. In a small firm, this can be done quite effectively via a series of group discussions based around questions such as 'How would we describe our culture to an outsider?' or 'What are the five things that we value most?'. In a larger firm, some formal questionnaire will have to be devised. However, in my experience, once the data from this has been gathered, it is usually still necessary to refine it through some kind of discussion process.

In order for the firm to benefit from defining its values and culture, it is important that the conclusions reached be written down in a short, simple form that can be related easily to the SWOT analysis. The strategic direction normally begins to emerge when the two are put together.

2.3 Preference for evolution or revolution

A key part of any firm's culture is how quickly and how radically it is able to change. Most lawyers are rather conservative and do not welcome change of any kind. Many law firms also have quite flat partnership structures, which can slow down processes of change. If one simply accepts the natural drag created by these phenomena, change in a law firm can easily become so slow that it grinds to a halt. This will not create an environment in which new strategies can be developed or implemented.

In order to counterbalance this natural conservatism, those responsible for developing the strategy must create some sense of urgency. All involved should be made to feel that things cannot remain as they are and that there is some kind of deadline for change. This might be an important milestone, such as an annual partnership retreat or the end of a financial year. Needless to say, if real threats come into view (eg, client losses or reduced business), law firm leaders must seize these chances to force the partnership to shake off complacency. Leaders should never waste the opportunities that arise from a genuine crisis.

The election of new leaders often creates a climate in which more radical change is possible. Such opportunities should also not be squandered. The moment when a new leader is elected is the moment with the greatest potential for significant change, provided that the possibility of such change has been clearly flagged up in the election process and provided that the new leader moves swiftly to bring it about. New leaders must hit the ground running and use appropriate symbols to show that this is real change.

Having said all of this, unless the firm is in a really dire position or the key partners in the firm are really gung-ho, it is highly unlikely that a law firm partnership can change as radically and as quickly as most major corporations. Law firm leaders who try to go further and faster than other key opinion formers within their firms wish them to tend not to survive. Even if you are a strong leader and you have clear ideas about where the firm should go, it is therefore important that you create at the outset a core team of the firm's most influential and successful partners to help you to define the pace and scope of change. It is unwise to make bold statements such as 'things in this firm will never be the same again' unless you are confident about your ability to deliver on them. This is even more the case now that the affairs of law firms are subject to considerable media scrutiny.

2.4 Competitive environment in which the firm operates

First you must work out who your direct competitors are. Most law firms are part of a relatively small group of competing firms trying to do the same things with the same clients in a similar way. That is the group you really want to understand very well.

You should be as precise and clear as possible, using hard facts and figures, about how your firm measures up against its competitors. A lot of data is needed for this, including number of partners, number of fee earners, total number of staff, profitability and key clients. This should be recorded in a consistent format and verified as far as possible. If it can be achieved without breaching relevant antitrust regulations or other professional duties, cross-check what you come up with by engaging with your competitors. Also, see what information can be gathered with the assistance of those who have had close involvement with competitors, whether as partners, employees or clients.

Your clients can help a great deal here too. Give the best of them a list of who you think your competitors are and see whether they agree. You will often be surprised to find that a client might regard a firm that you think of as lower tier as a significant competitor, whereas another firm you might regard as one of your usual competitors might not be seen in that way by most of your clients. Once you have a clear picture of the competition, you can begin to work out a plan for differentiating your firm. This is a key requirement in today's competitive environment.

2.5 The people who should be involved in the process

Every firm contains a relatively small number of opinion formers and leaders. A successful law firm leader tries to engage all of them in the strategic planning process, even if some of them are difficult to deal with. Any strategy that is developed by a small clique and then presented in a near-final form to the partnership at large is doomed. A key benefit of strategic planning is the involvement of all key stakeholders in the process. They frequently benefit as much from participating in developing the strategy as they do from trying to implement it.

As explained above, as well as creating an internal group to develop your firm's strategy, you also need external input at all stages of strategic planning. The most important constituency is your existing or potential clients. If asked, and presented with the information in a digestible form, they are often more than willing to help a firm develop its strategy. In fact, they are often flattered to be asked and are much more likely to use the firm in the future if they are made to feel involved in its strategic planning.

Where possible, client feedback on a law firm's strategy is best presented face to face. Ideally, the firm should invite key clients to a strategy retreat to get their frank and immediate reactions to the firm's proposed strategy. The more open you are with your clients, the more likely they are to give you worthwhile input.

There are, of course, many other external players who may be involved in strategic planning. Most firms have external auditors and it is certainly worth asking them. In addition, friendly firms in other jurisdictions with which you regularly deal would normally be happy to share their experiences. And again, they would be flattered to be asked for their advice. You can also ask partners who have recently retired from competing firms, or clients' general counsel who are 'between jobs' and looking for an opportunity to earn some money by undertaking a short-term strategy project. Whether you want to seek further advice from an external adviser is very much a question of taste. In my experience, different firms take radically different views on this.

If you do decide to consult an external adviser, you have a choice between going to one of the various consultancy firms that specialise in advising law firms or seeking out a particular individual with prior law firm experience. This may be someone such as a former finance director of a larger law firm, who can become part of your team for a limited period while a change process is developed and implemented. Both kinds of help are readily available, so it is a good idea to explore each one before deciding what kind of external input (if any) to get. However, the key thing to remember is that the strategy must be your firm's, not one given to the firm by its external adviser. Advisers can add significant value, but they cannot do the job of those running the firm. In the end, all successful strategies are home grown and must have clear owners within the firm.

3. Deciding on the type of firm you want to be

Having gathered all the building blocks together, it is time to decide on the direction you want to take. This will involve consideration of four key questions:

- What is the right model for your firm?
- How should your firm be structured?
- How will your firm make decisions?
- How will your firm know if its strategy is working?

3.1 What is the right model for your firm?

The scale, focus and infrastructure of law firms vary enormously, depending on the breadth of practice they plan to encompass. In this context, it is helpful to try to place any firm into one of the following categories:

- International firm – one that does business in a substantial number of different countries around the world and has a physical presence in quite a few of them;
- Regional firm – one that does business in, and has offices in, a number of neighbouring countries and focuses specifically on those;
- National firm – one that restricts itself to practising the laws of a specific jurisdiction and seeks to service multi-jurisdictional work by collaborating with friendly law firms in other jurisdictions;
- Local firm – one that restricts its activities to a particular part of a country;
- Specialist firm – one that specialises in a particular type of legal service or a particular industrial or commercial sector, but perhaps does that across a wide geographic area;
- Focus firm – one that focuses solely on a handful of key clients and seeks to present packages that are tailored exclusively to the needs of those clients; or
- Virtual firm – one that is in reality an alliance of various different service providers, without full economic or structural integration but united under a single brand to provide clients with a total service.

No firm can be all of the above. It is important to make choices and differentiate yourself from others. This also gives your partners and staff a much clearer understanding of what they must do to compete successfully. No strategy can be implemented successfully by people who do not know how they should respond to a particular competitive situation. The test here is: 'If x happens, will everyone in the firm know that the response should be y?'

In deciding what model you are and want to 'be', you must look hard at the answers given to some of the questions covered in the previous sections. But, as in so many other things, it is also important to look to your closest competitors and see what kind of firm they are.

Once again, I would recommend completing this exercise in writing and seeing clearly how you measure up against your competitors before deciding on the areas in which you want to compete. Real data and a recognition of harsh realities must underpin any successful strategy.

This is not a 'battle of the models'. One model is not going to succeed more than the others in all possible cases. Each model can be equally successful (or otherwise), depending on how well aligned it is with the strengths and aspirations of the firm concerned. The key thing is to pick the right model, to stick with it and to be better at implementing and operating it than those other firms trying to do the same thing. This game awards prizes for perseverance.

3.2 How should your firm be structured?

The legal press is full of stories relating to law firm structures. For example, we read repeatedly of the apparent differences between 'lockstep' partnerships, where profits are divided according to a rigid formula related to length of service, and 'eat what you kill' partnerships, in which the top performers earn much more than the average partner. In my experience, relatively few partnerships operate either system in a pure form. This is because, beneath the surface, there are many possible variations on each basic model. These include 'modified' lockstep, in which partner remuneration generally goes in bands and there are 'gates' through which partners have to progress in order to move from one band to another.

While profit distribution is an important issue, it is not the only one to be addressed under the heading of structure. Others include the following:

- Will the firm be a single partnership or a series of connected partnerships?
- Will partners' liability be limited or unlimited?
- Will there be any external capital or borrowings?
- Will the firm own other assets (eg, the land or buildings that the firm occupies), which imply a need for significantly more capital, or will capital requirements be kept to a minimum (eg, leasing office space and financing the firm's operations largely from retained earnings)?
- What contribution will partners have to make when they join the partnership, how will this be financed and on what basis will they be able to withdraw capital when they leave?
- Will partners receive a pension?
- Will restrictive covenants apply, limiting what partners can do after they leave?
- How are partners to be admitted and expelled?
- Is there a retirement age?

Once the nature of the relationship between partners has been determined, there will obviously be other issues to be addressed relating to the structure and organisation of the fee-earning departments (eg, different practice groups or different offices) and the support functions (eg, IT, HR, finance). Each particular type of partnership structure will tend to encourage the firm to adopt a specific approach to the organisation of each of these other areas.

It is generally necessary for all partners in a law firm to devote the majority of their time to fee earning, since the partners are generally the most important fee earners and since their credibility as practitioners typically depends on them continuing to work 'at the front line'. However, in a well-run firm, many partners will also need to take on other responsibilities – whether those are leadership roles (eg, senior partner, managing partner, practice group leader, office head) or responsibilities for other areas (eg, know-how, business development, recruitment, innovation, finance). In a small firm it is often possible for a single partner to take on more than one of these wider roles, but a key to success will be to ensure that each role has clear responsibilities and targets assigned to it, and that there is proper control over the amount of time that a partner spends on such an additional responsibility (eg, an agreement that he or she will spend only 15% of his or her time on the relevant additional role).

All of these matters must be considered and dealt with as part of an overall package that is developed with the firm's strategy in mind. Consistency, clarity and transparency are extremely important. For law firms, in many ways, structure, governance and strategy go hand in hand.

3.3 How will your firm make decisions?

Most law firms are partnerships. The partnership model requires a degree of consensus. This can be a good thing because it creates a strong sense of cohesion and limits the risk of serious mistakes being made as a result of one person's misguided ideas. However, without care, consensus can become a recipe for paralysis.

Part of the firm's strategy needs to relate to how it is going to make business-like decisions while carrying the bulk of the partnership with it. As already mentioned, this is best done by a process leadership election. The elected leaders can then stand on a clear strategic platform. In a democratic partnership, leaders who have a clear mandate and have espoused a strong set of strategic priorities will have a much better chance of implementing the strategy. As in so many other cases, alignment with the firm's culture and values is also important. Furthermore, if you are considering contested elections (which are a good idea), you must have a plan for retaining the losers (which is not easy). Similar issues arise when a leader's term expires, if he or she is not eligible for reappointment. In both cases it is best for the new leadership to propose a specific role for the loser or the former leader which would typically involve some external-facing responsibility (eg, dealing with important clients or new jurisdictions), which can be quite high profile and rewarding.

In my experience, most law firms are very happy to talk to other firms about the ways in which they make decisions. There is no need to reinvent the wheel. Decision-making processes that work well in one firm are quite likely to be suitable for a similar firm. It is well worth exploring how other firms deal with these things before making a decision in respect of your own firm.

A matrix decision-making structure works well in many different contexts. The starting point for this is to recognise that a 'normal' partner wears three different hats: as an owner, a manager and a producer. Distinguishing when the partner performs these three functions makes choosing a decision-making structure much easier. In many firms, all partners are simultaneously members of practice groups (eg, the corporate group) and of sector groups (eg, mining), office or regional groups (eg, Frankfurt or Asia). In this regard, each partner must also be clear about the capacity in which he or she is acting whenever he or she does something.

Most partners expect to be able to decide on the admission of new partners and to be able to select the overall leadership of the firm. These two things are therefore best dealt with through firm-wide votes. Once elected, the leadership should be left to lead. But in order to avoid a large and expensive infrastructure at the centre of the firm, it is a good idea to delegate as much responsibility as possible to individual operating units within the firm. These might either be different practice groups or sector groups, or different office or regional groups. Localised decision making within the constraints of an overall strategy is likely to outperform a more centralised structure.

3.4 How will your firm know whether its strategy is working?

Although the process of developing a strategy is valuable in itself, clearly the main aim should be to ensure that the strategy is implemented and achieves the desired results. This does not mean that any strategy will provide you with a reliable blueprint that can be implemented in full. I have never been involved in developing any strategy that met that very rigorous test. However, a good strategy should provide a clear starting point for your firm's evolution and be capable of being adapted in the light of experience so that it remains relevant and aspirational, yet achievable.

The first thing to do, of course, is to write the strategy down in a simple and communicable fashion. The choice of words is really important. No strategy can be implemented effectively unless all those concerned have a common understanding of what it is. Spending a significant amount of time choosing the words you are going to use and testing them on others is thus a good investment. Words that can be understood equally well and in a common way in many different linguistic and cultural contexts will add a lot, especially if people from more than one country or with more than one linguistic or cultural background are members of the same firm.

A strategy is more likely to be implemented by those who feel that they have shared in its development. For this reason, it is recommended that whatever you come up with be shared as a draft with a wide range of people before it is finalised. Ensure that your partners and other stakeholders feel that they have had some work to do in developing the strategy, rather than thinking they are just being presented with a *fait accompli*. Remember that lawyers are not the only important people in law firms. Support staff are also vital. Sharing the strategy with them and giving them a sense of ownership will help implementation. The same goes for clients and other stakeholders.

Good strategies should have clear, measurable targets. Where possible, these should be hard numbers. These can be checked when the strategy is adopted and re-checked every six months, for example, to see whether progress is being made. The numbers concerned might include turnover, profit margin, number of clients, number of partners, number of staff, percentage of business derived from particular types of work and so on. In order to ensure a level playing field, somebody reliable and impartial should be asked to generate all of the numbers involved on a consistent basis and at regular intervals. In many firms, this task is given to the finance director or office manager.

Allocate responsibility for each part of the strategy to a different person and make its implementation a key part of his or her responsibilities. Arrange a formal meeting with that person when the strategy is being implemented to agree what he or she will do, how this will be done and over what timescale in order to achieve the target that he or she has been given. Record these discussions and share the results with the individual concerned. Performance in this area should be considered in annual performance reviews. Also ensure that there are regular progress meetings in which the measures of performance (ie, the numbers mentioned above) are presented and agreed, and in which conclusions may be drawn about what should happen next.

It is essential that any strategy be pursued consistently over a long period of time (eg, several years). If, during this period, it becomes necessary to change the strategy, that change should be articulated and explained clearly and all documents recording the strategy should be updated. If the strategy is redrawn after the first few years because it has not worked, it is extremely important that the reasons for the previous failure be fully understood and a significantly different approach adopted the next time around. Your colleagues and your staff will ignore future strategic planning activities that you seek to instigate if they feel that previous efforts in this field have been unrewarding. It is therefore recommended that each significant step during the normal management and development of your firm be tied to the relevant strategic objective, so that everyone can see how it is being driven by the strategy.

In order to avoid unnecessary confusion, if you end up doing something that is not aligned with the strategy (eg, in taking advantage of an unexpected opportunity or in responding to an unforeseen problem), ensure that you explain to everyone that this particular thing was not envisaged in the strategy and how you plan to adapt the strategy to accommodate it.

When assessing the success of your firm, make good use of external directories and rankings. A good strategy should result in your firm moving up the rankings. If that does not happen after a few years, it is important to step back and ask why.

4.   **Testing your strategy against the challenges faced by your firm**
Having developed a draft strategy, it is a good idea to see how it meets some of the strategic challenges that your firm faces. A strategy that does not help you to address these in a realistic fashion is unlikely to be worth the paper it is written on.

Each firm must decide what its principal challenges are. However, they might include the following:
- coping with multi-jurisdictional matters;
- staying 'lean and mean';

- remaining competitive;
- attracting and retaining key clients and key people; and
- managing growth.

4.1 Coping with multi-jurisdictional matters

Nowadays, almost every law firm in the world has to deal with matters involving more than one jurisdiction. However, no firm is physically present in every jurisdiction on the planet. Every firm is therefore required to develop a strategy that will, to a greater or lesser extent, allow it to cope with matters involving places in which it is not present. Traditionally, most firms choose whom to work with in other jurisdictions on a case-by-case basis. However, clients are increasingly unconvinced by this approach. In my opinion, it will become more and more necessary for firms to have clear preferences about whom to work with and the formal or informal alliances with firms in other jurisdictions that are important for their business. This can be accomplished through membership of one or more international networks, or in a more bespoke fashion by developing good friends in key jurisdictions.

Most successful firms want to position their partners as the 'trusted advisers' of key clients. In today's globalised world, this cannot be achieved unless key partners have some meaningful comparative legal knowledge. It is less a case of giving a formal legal opinion on whether something works in a particular jurisdiction than having a good general feel for what the key issues will be in different parts of the world and being able to give a client a sensible overview of them. Most clients value a 'helicopter view'. This, of course, must be combined with the ability to work together on an integrated basis with locally qualified lawyers when the need arises.

In developing their strategies, firms should think carefully about their international network and clearly designate who within the partnership is going to have primary responsibility for international relations. Participation in relevant international gatherings, such as the Annual Meeting of the International Bar Association, will obviously help greatly in this regard. However, this is a significant role that takes up a substantial amount of time. It is unlikely that any firm will succeed in developing and implementing a truly international strategy without allocating sufficient time and resources to the process. It must also be addressed in a focused way that avoids individual partners doing their own thing.

4.2 Staying lean and mean

All clients now want more for less. For every client the cost of legal services is an overhead, and all boards, chief executives and finance directors are trying to reduce these. As a result, it is essential that any law firm strategy incorporates a means of delivering more for less.

Efficiency is the key. This can be achieved only with well-developed skills and systems for the management of people and projects, together with the careful management of costs. The biggest costs in any law firm are the people. Headcount management must therefore underpin the firm's strategy. It is important that the strategy be translated into some firm headcount limits, and that someone be responsible for ensuring that the firm adheres to these.

Most firms manage headcount by setting a limit on the total number of fee earners (designed to ensure that they are all working at full capacity) and then establishing a ratio of fee earners to support staff (eg, 0.75% support staff to one fee earner, meaning that if you have 20 fee earners, you will have 15 support staff). If possible, the support staff ratios should be broken down further to indicate what percentage should be personal assistants and what percentage should be in other support functions (eg, HR, IT, business development).

A constant source of inefficiency in law firms is the tendency for support functions to be performed by busy partners in their spare time rather than to be entrusted to well-qualified and experienced professional and support staff. A modern law firm cannot be successful without bringing on board very high-quality non-legal staff and empowering them to manage all of those things within the firm that do not have to be undertaken by lawyers. The more efficiently that a firm runs its support functions, the more likely that it will be able to implement its strategy.

A key support function is finance. Strategies have to be translated into business plans, and business plans have to be supported by budgets. Law firm budgeting is an underdeveloped art, but it is essential in strategy development and implementation. Like many things connected with law firms, the more you do it, the better you will get at it.

Another key issue is investment in technology. Well-judged use of technology can make law firms much more efficient, but unwise experiments can cost them dearly. A business strategy should include a strategy for technology as a key component. Law firms can also take a leaf out their clients' books when it comes to focusing on their core business.

A large number of firms outsource non-essential functions in both the legal and support spheres. Imaginative use of external providers or outsourcing options can add a lot to a firm's strategy and improve its chances of maintaining profitability in a competitive environment. The same applies to placing resources in less costly locations. This can, of course, be done internationally, but it is also an option domestically. For example, a modern firm does not necessarily need to situate all of its people in the most expensive part of town.

4.3   Remaining competitive

As previously mentioned, you cannot achieve a competitive advantage unless you know who your competitors are and how your firm can be differentiated from them. Write down the names of your main competitors and make sure that everyone in the firm knows who they are. Get some data on them and record their rankings in directories and elsewhere, and compare these with your own. Do this every year. Check to see whether new competitors have appeared (eg, because of mergers or because of the kind of external investment in the legal sector now permitted in the United Kingdom) or whether previous competitors have disappeared (eg, due to insolvency or a radical change of strategy).

In order to become more competitive, law firms normally need to become more innovative. Innovation can take the form of improvements in how existing services are delivered or the creation of an entirely new service. When attempting to encourage innovation, you should be equally open to both forms and should specifically seek out and reward internally generated ideas, however unrealistic they might at first seem. Brainstorming has real value. Make one of your partners responsible for innovation and give him or her the means to test innovative ideas in an environment in which people will not be blamed if they do not work.

One innovation that regularly comes up in the context of law firm strategy is the 'commoditisation' or 'industrialisation' of the law. In general, legal services and processes are all susceptible to standardisation. The more that this occurs, the more that the product you are selling becomes a commodity that can be produced more efficiently and therefore on better terms for the client and the firm. Explain to all of your staff what commoditisation really involves and seek a constructive dialogue with them and your clients as to how more of it can take place in the firm, and so achieve a win-win result for all.

Another area relating to commoditisation is the 'unbundling' of legal services. This involves taking the various components of a matter and looking at each separately. In this way it may be seen whether all the work involved should be done by the same firm or whether some parts can be diverted to a different (perhaps cheaper) firm.

With regard to both commoditisation and unbundling, it is important to have regular, mature discussions with each client about how much these processes might relate to their work and what the benefits to the client and the firm might be. Solution B may be less perfect than Solution A, but if it is also cheaper, a sophisticated client and an innovative law firm may nevertheless decide to opt for it. Training your clients to make better use of your services will improve profitability, increase client loyalty and motivate your partners and staff.

A major obstacle to improved competitiveness derives from those barriers within law firms that stop people from working together as effectively as they might. Most firms that I have ever dealt with contain a number of distinct tribal groups. These comprise people who work together in a very intense way, but interact much less with the rest of the firm. These are sometimes called 'silos'. Although there are some advantages to working in a silo (those in the team know how to work well together and know who is doing what), they are often a major barrier to improved efficiency and the transfer of good practice. All firms have to try to break down silos by forcing people to work together across them. Multi-disciplinary client service groups or industrial sector groups can help a lot in this process.

The other competitive threats that all firms face are the ups and downs of the wider economy. When there is a recession, there is less work for lawyers and law firms have to adapt quickly to changing market conditions. Therefore, any effective law firm leader has to keep a close eye on the weekly indicators of the performance of the wider economy and look constantly to see how the firm's strategy and staffing must adapt to take account of any shifts.

4.4   Attracting and retaining key clients and key people
It is often said that the most valuable assets of any law firm 'leave the building and go home every night'. Without good people, you cannot have a good firm. Those

people must be present at every level, both legal and support, or you will not create a premium brand for your firm.

Of course, good people like to be treated well. This does not mean that they want to have an easy life. Typically, they want to be stretched and developed, to undertake interesting work in a reasonable environment and to feel motivated to achieve their best. In the service sector, it is by no means easy to achieve the right balance in this regard, because all service organisations have to respond well to the (often unreasonable) demands of their clients.

People sometimes ask, "What comes first – good people or good clients?" Does your firm attract excellent people because you have great clients for which the best people like to work, or do you attract good clients because you have excellent people whom clients want to seek out? In my experience, the answer is normally "a bit of both". This is a field in which you really want to create a virtuous circle in which you are constantly adding excellent people to the organisation at every level, and at the same time constantly adding excellent clients. Getting the best people and the best clients takes a lot of time and effort. Any strategy must include those two elements working in tandem.

In the past, some firms appeared to overstretch their staff for the sake of achieving an excellent service for their clients. One sometimes got the feeling that whenever a client said, "Jump!" the firm replied, "How high and how quickly?" I must tell you that this approach will not be the foundation of a successful strategy.

Ensure your best clients fully understand what you are trying to do with the development and motivation of your people, and are willing to help by taking a mature view and making your best people feel loved and wanted. Any sensible client will respond well to an invitation to invest some time and effort in the long-term development of your human resources. Ask them regularly for feedback on your staff so that they can help you to reward and develop those with the greatest potential and at the same time weed out those who are underperforming. Clients will respect you more if you sometimes say no to an unreasonable request in order to protect your staff, and your staff will perform better if you openly share your strategy for attracting and retaining the best clients.

The very best partners have achieved the status of being trusted advisers to their key clients. Young lawyers rarely develop this skill on their own account. They have to be trained suitably and presented with good role models. Clients can help lawyers to make this transition.

A key issue for all clients is returning something to the community, via community investment projects, pro bono initiatives and so on. Law firms can gain a lot from encouraging their best younger people to work alongside their best clients in projects of this kind. It can be very motivating for all concerned.

4.5   Managing growth

Many firms get into difficulties by expanding too quickly. Uncontrolled growth is always a bad thing. On the other hand, as the Chinese proverb apparently says, "The bicycle that does not move forward falls over". Therefore, growth and development are essential.

You cannot achieve growth without investment. Investment is tricky for most firms because they generally do not have any external capital and normally distribute all of their profits each year. Up to now, almost all law firms have been a pyramid, with significantly more people at the bottom (ie, the junior levels) than at the top (ie, partners). Therefore, once a firm is established, growth is normally organic, meaning that more people are hired at the bottom of the pyramid every year and as a result, most of the higher levels grow due to the promotion of people from the more junior levels. Thus, setting a target for entry-level fee earner recruitment is an important activity for all law firms. In my experience, there are normally plenty of excellent young people to be hired at entry level and you have the best chance of producing successful future partners by 'growing your own'.

However, this strategy is viable only if firms continue in a traditional pyramid configuration. Some commentators have suggested that firms might become 'diamond-shaped' because clients are generally less willing to pay for the training and development of younger staff and want fewer younger people working on their matters. If this proves correct, firms will inevitably have to grow more through lateral hiring at more senior levels. Well-thought-out lateral hiring can greatly increase a firm's success. However, there are some major issues here regarding the integration of laterals. Cost is also an issue: new laterals must be paid immediately, but they will take time to become fully productive. A great deal of research has been done in this field, showing that the most successful firms are significantly better at lateral hiring than the less successful ones.

The bigger a firm becomes, the more bureaucracy creeps in and the more the firm needs to adopt tougher management structures and internal policies and procedures. Such developments are a natural part of the evolution of most firms, but the changes they involve require careful management. There is plenty of experience available in making the transition from a small organisation to a mid-sized or even large one, and law firm leaders would be well advised to familiarise themselves with this.

Bigger, more successful firms tend to attract bigger and more complex clients. Managing relationships with large, sophisticated clients takes a great deal of skill, time and effort. Your staff will need to be trained to do this and need to see it as one of their key responsibilities. Regular client meetings that are properly documented and followed up should play a key role in the firm's growth and development.

Professional rules relating to conflicts of interest force law firms to make choices about the clients for which they will act. These choices must be addressed strategically. Therefore, underpinning any strategy for growth in the client base must be a strategy for targeting preferred clients and avoiding taking on clients which will not help you to advance your strategic development. This process cannot be left to the individual initiative of particular partners. It requires collective decision making and responsibility.

5.   Some final thoughts

- All law firms need a strategy.
- Every strategy must be rooted in reality, but also have an aspirational element.

- Develop your strategy in a rigorous manner, but do not allow the process to drag on. In most firms, this means completing the development of a strategy within six months.
- Write down your strategy and ensure that it is effectively communicated, both internally and externally.
- Review your strategy regularly.

Strategic challenges for law firms in the 21st century

Alan Hodgart
Huron Consulting Group

1.   The starting point

The global legal market has undergone enormous structural and operational changes over the last 25 years. The competitive pressures behind these changes show no signs of abating. In fact, the signs are that they will increase. These pressures are ultimately client driven, even though the actions behind them come from law firms. It is clients that decide whether to accept what law firms offer as they seek to improve their competitiveness.

The changes in the last quarter of a century have been striking. At the start of the 1990s, the legal profession was focused primarily on technical proficiency and operated in a very benign state of competitiveness. Clients did move between firms from time to time, but many used one firm to provide all (or most) of their legal requirements. Firms did very little marketing, if any. Indeed, many marketing activities were not allowed by professional association regulations. Firms billed on hourly rates with little justification to clients for what had been done other than the legal opinion that had been produced. Legal advice generally extended to interpretations of the law rather than commercial answers based on those laws. Law firm management was really office administration and partners acted autonomously in regard to their clients and work. Whether they were involved with business clients or private clients, most partners were generalists: within these broad categories an individual partner would provide advice across a wide range of legal areas. Becoming a partner was effectively a job for life. Demand and supply patterns varied little across the profession other than in some specific high-value areas in a limited number of markets (mainly New York and London). Finally, firms at the start of the 1990s were small compared to today's, even in major markets such as the United States and the United Kingdom (see Tables 3 and 4 below).

Today, the degree of competition varies around the world. In some markets it is intense, while in others it is still developing. Nevertheless, there is agreement about the general trend. In the more competitive markets many firms are run as professional businesses, with a central management with a strategic and operational management role. In some firms management directs operations tightly, while in others it takes a more collegiate approach. But the move towards a more managed environment is clearly underway. Strategies and business plans are becoming established and the autonomy of partners is reducing. Firms seek through these plans to differentiate themselves within their chosen market sectors, and partners are expected to follow them. As firms seek to build market share within their areas of strategic focus, market and business development have become high priorities. Partner performance management systems abound. Increasingly, partners are also required to achieve specified performance levels or face reductions in earnings – or even departure from the firm.

While many firms are still 'full service' in one sense, this relates more to the legal requirements of broad sectors of the market than the ability to provide every possible legal service to anyone. Firms now compete aggressively with each other, focusing on service quality, client relationships and price. Greater attention is being given to managing client relationships. Firms are aware that their competitiveness depends as much on the quality of the service provided as on technical proficiency. In fact, clients believe that there are many areas of law in which it is not possible to distinguish firms which are at the same level in the market (a peer group) by their level of technical skill. In these cases service quality and price are seen as the primary differentiators. A strong relationship with a client also allows a lawyer to understand better its service preferences.

It is a moot point whether clients or a few law firms drove the initial market changes. Nevertheless, the market for legal services has changed dramatically. Clients, especially business clients, have become more demanding. They are prepared to change firms if they feel they are not getting value for money or the required expertise. They want greater certainty over pricing. They perceive the strengths of various firms and allocate their work based on those perceptions. Hence firms, and lawyers within firms, are required to specialise more. Clients now want depth of knowledge in areas that are important to them: they do not see generalists as able to provide that depth.

An understanding of how the market structure for legal services is changing is still not widespread and is not fully accepted. All competitive industries go through a process of segmentation and the legal industry is no exception. It is happening to the legal market at the moment. Each segment has a somewhat different set of competitive characteristics from the others. Some segments focus on the value of the work – that is, the value perceived by the client. So large and complex M&A deals and capital markets work, both perceived as high value, have become dominated by New York and London firms which have focused on building their competitiveness in these areas. The lower-value segments, such as insurance claims, are dominated by smaller firms. Clients here see the work as price driven.

Firms that structure their business model correctly can succeed in a particular segment and be quite profitable. But the structure for one segment is not necessarily appropriate for another. Hence, firms need to choose carefully the core segments in which they will compete, such that their competitive requirements are similar or overlap, and reject others whose competitive requirements are too different.

Segmentation takes many different forms. It may revolve around certain types of client or practice area (or both), and around the value that clients place on certain types of work. In this way, the leading New York and London firms have focused on the large transactions segment (M&A and capital markets). This tends to involve the leading investment banks and Global 500 companies. This is therefore a segment defined by a certain type of work, a certain type of client and a high value. These firms have capabilities in many other service areas, but they tend to package these around their core clients and core work.

Other segments are at the other end of the corporate spectrum. These focus on smaller companies, where the client is the owner. Here, cost effectiveness is the defining feature. Some firms choose to compete on the basis of in-depth industry knowledge, using it to shape their advice and service delivery to clients. Over time, these firms will lose clients that do not operate within the chosen industries and not win any new clients outside those sectors. However, many firms have not understood this. These firms also tend to cover far too many industries with unrelated competitive requirements and so remain generalists. Segmentation is not yet widely understood within the legal market. As we note below, it is a major challenge for the future.

Nevertheless, as a result of these changes, we now have some very large firms with extensive international coverage. Twenty-five years ago, many did not think that this would be possible. As in most other industries, competition is leading to the growth of some firms and the consolidation of work around fewer, larger firms in each segment. Most have achieved this through a combination of aggressive organic growth supported by mergers and team hires. Table 1 sets out the top 10 largest law firms in the world: all of them have in excess of 1,300 lawyers.

Table 1: Top 10 law firms globally

Rank	Firm name	Number of lawyers
1	Baker & McKenzie	3,738
2	DLA Piper	3,576
3	Clifford Chance	2,912
4	Hogan Lovells	2,601
5	Allen & Overy	2,529
6	Linklaters	2,520
7	Jones Day	2,502
8	Freshfields Bruckhaus Deringer	2,232
9	Garrigues	2,121
10	Mayer Brown	1,969

Source: Legal Business Global 100, 2011

In the last three years there have been three 'true' transatlantic mergers between firms both in excess of 500 lawyers prior to the merger. In the same time period some very small firms in continental Europe have also merged with US firms (see Table 2).

Table 2: Transatlantic mergers

Date	Firm 1	Size	Firm 2	Size
January 2008	Paul Hastings	1,125	Smeets Haas Wolff	27
September 2008	Orrick Herrington & Sutcliffe	1,100	Hölters & Elsing	51
May 2009	McGuireWoods	900	Grundberg Mocatta Rakison	36
May 2010	Lovells	1,421	Hogan & Hartson	1,111
September 2010	Sonnenschein Nath Rosenthal	655	Denton Wilde Sapte	600
October 2010	Baker & McKenzie	3,950	Findling Collin Fessmann	15
January 2011	Squire Sanders & Dempsey	761	Hammonds	500

Source: Altman Weil, Inc

This growth is also shown at the top of the UK and US markets, the source of most international growth. Tables 3 and 4 compare the average size of the top 10 firms in both jurisdictions in 1992 and 2011. The average increase in the United Kingdom is 254% (Table 3) and in the United States is 208% (Table 4).

Table 3: Size of top 10 UK firms in 1992 and 2011

Rank 1992	Firm name	Number of lawyers	Rank 2011	Firm name	Number of lawyers
1	Clifford Chance	1,168	1	DLA Piper	3,576
2	Linklaters & Paines	718	2	Clifford Chance	2,912
3	Freshfields	645	3	Linklaters	2,520
4	Lovell White Durrant	616	4	Freshfields	2,232
5	Slaughter and May	567	5	Allen & Overy	2,529
6	Allen & Overy	543	6	Hogan Lovells	2,601
7	Simmons & Simmons	474	7	Norton Rose	1,737
8	Norton Rose	470	8	Herbert Smith	1,347
9	Herbert Smith	446	9	Slaughter and May	728
10	Nabarro	400	10	Eversheds	1,228
	Average size	605		Average size	2,141

Table 4: Size of top 10 US firms in 1992 and 2011

Rank 1992	Firm name	Number of lawyers		Rank 2011	Firm name	Number of lawyers
1	Skadden, Arps	996		1	Baker & McKenzie	3,738
2	Baker & McKenzie	1,582		2	Skadden, Arps	1,859
3	Jones Day	1,147		3	DLA Piper	3,348
4	Gibson, Dunn & Crutcher	617		4	Latham & Watkins	1,931
5	Shearman & Sterling	550		5	Hogan Lovells	2,363
6	Sullivan & Cromwell	352		6	Kirkland & Ellis	1,379
7	Davis Polk & Wardwell	410		7	Jones Day	2,502
8	Weil, Gotshal & Manges	545		8	Sidley Austin	1,538
9	Latham & Watkins	574		9	White & Case	1,814
10	Cleary, Gottlieb	426		10	Greenberg Traurig	1,721
	Average size	720			Average size	2,219

In terms of international capability, 23 of the top 25 firms in the United Kingdom now have two or more offices outside the United Kingdom. All top 25 US firms have two or more offices outside the United States.

As a consequence, both scale and international capability are seen as important differentiators in certain types of work and by specific types of client. This does not mean that smaller firms cannot compete effectively in many areas. But the shift towards scale and international capability has reduced the areas in which they can do so.

Some firms are building close relationships with similar, more domestically focused firms in other countries as a way of competing, while others have become members of global alliances. A number of large firms use their scale to reduce costs and maintain profit levels. This is a recent trend and has not yet had a major effect on legal markets. However, it may become a threat to smaller firms in the future.

Price competition has been a feature of the low-value end of the legal market for some time. But in recent years it has crept up the value chain. It has always lurked in the background, but the recent downturn has seen it come quickly to the fore. Clients have long complained about the pricing model of law firms. The hourly rate model, leading to a cost–plus approach, has for a long time irked small and large clients alike. Although most businesses are required to state the price of their product or service upfront, and so manage their own costs, law firms claim this is too difficult and have billed by the hour recorded for the work. While discounts and special arrangements exist, the hourly rate pricing model continues to dominate the legal industry.

This is changing. Clients are demanding more certainty in the final price of legal work. They accept that they cannot always have a fixed price upfront, but they now expect a law firm to be able at least to estimate a price or, where that is difficult, estimate stage by stage. Clients increasingly do not accept that it is impossible to have an idea of the final price before the work is undertaken. They see law firms advertising themselves as experts in their field. From a client's perspective, if they are experts then they should be able to estimate a price and predict what might cause the estimate to vary. The hourly rate model also gives firms no incentive to become more efficient. Several approaches to pricing are now in use, but the general move is towards a clearer structure in advance of the client agreeing to a firm undertaking work. This at least moves some of the risk onto the firm if the work takes more time than has been estimated in the price quotation.

The problem for the vast majority of law firms is twofold. Partners do not have experience of pricing models other than hourly rates, and they have not been trained to manage the cost of an engagement to a fixed price (or estimate) so that clients' price expectations are met and the required level of profit is generated. Partners are generally not aware of the profit margin required from their work. Neither are they aware of the cost structures and profit margins of different staff levels. Under an hourly rate, this matters less because cost is largely passed onto the client. Discounting reduces profits, but most firms make an allowance for this in their budget.

Many firms around the world are struggling with this issue and will continue to do so. Clients face budget constraints and must achieve significant efficiencies: they expect law firms to do the same. Some lawyers think this issue is just driven by the downturn, but client interviews suggest otherwise. Clients accept that should demand once again significantly exceed supply (as it did between 2005 and 2008), then some return to hourly rate pricing might take place. However, the general view is that this is some way off. Even if it does arrive, clients will continue to put pressure on law firms before and after it. This issue will only become more important over the next few years.

Many firms are moving to a more strategic approach to their business and in recent years have improved their management processes. However, most have still not started the transition from the old model. Even in the more competitive markets, firms still have not moved much in this direction. Fewer have done so in markets where competition is not yet at a high level. Nevertheless, the current structural change in the legal market requires a major change in how firms think about how their business is structured and managed. This is a worldwide trend.

2. Continuing the challenge in the 21st century

In order to compete, law firms of all types must develop a strategic management approach to their business. The need for this will continue in all jurisdictions and at all levels.

The critical strategic challenge is to achieve and then maintain strategic leadership. This should be the highest priority for firms, no matter what the market position in which they wish to compete. There are three components to strategic leadership:

- choosing a longer-term market position in which the firm wishes to compete;
- developing a strategy that will enhance the firm's competitiveness within its chosen market position; and
- ensuring that everyone in the firm understands the strategy, agrees with it and is working to achieve it.

Leadership is fundamental to all three components. Given the level of competitiveness that already operates in the global legal market, and the expectation that this will increase, strategic leadership is the most important requirement for success.

3. Clarity of strategic position

Law firms will face many important challenges over the next five to 10 years. Solving them will depend largely on firms knowing where they want to compete and their strategy for doing so. Market segmentation is the simple reason for this. Segmentation will continue apace, as it has in every other competitive industry, and will definitely change how law firms must compete and therefore operate. Those firms that grasp this change will be able to define a long-term competitive position. Those that don't will find life exceedingly difficult. Many will not survive.

A vital aspect of segmentation is how clients value specific types of advice. Some areas are of high importance to most businesses, while others hold a high value only for specific sectors. As noted, it is already becoming difficult for firms to provide services across sectors with widely differing competitive requirements. Perceptions of value range from the very high to the very low. The former requires a cost base that is vastly different from the latter, already meaning that firms cannot compete at all levels of value in the market. Those that try to do so are not optimising their profitability and tend not to be competitive in any segment. As many have already discovered, market share will be lost across the board. These firms will be forced to choose a narrower range in which to compete, merge with a firm that has already made a clear choice or close down.

The trend towards defining segments in the legal market, where the competitive conditions differ from other sectors, will continue. Clients will increasingly demand that firms which profess strength in a particular segment be able to justify it. Furthermore, clients' expectations of service value will toughen. We predict that the mid-value will disappear entirely in the long term. Clients see the advice they want as either at the higher or lower end of value. As a consequence, firms that want to compete in the mid-value market will lose some work to firms that meet higher expectations of value and some to others that provide work at a cost-effective level. Middle-ground firms will find that their market moves either upwards or downwards in value. A critical long-term strategic decision for firms is therefore whether they wish and are able to compete in the higher-value sector, or whether they need to focus primarily on the lower-value segment. This is not inconsistent with the high-value end of the market shrinking. A range of legal work will continue to come in below the highest level, with still a reasonable level of importance to clients.

This change in market structure requires some difficult strategic decisions to be taken. Firms will be forced to restrict the range of segments in which they compete. They must choose where they will be more or less competitive. The following factors, among others, will affect this choice:

- client types;
- industry sectors;
- range of practice areas;
- value level at which services are pitched; and
- geographical spread of the business.

Firms will choose various combinations of these in order to compete. The generalist firm – which seeks to present a wide range of service to a wide range of clients at a wide range of levels of value – will gradually disappear.

The strategic challenge today is that although the legal market is becoming segmented, this is still at an early stage. As a result, the vast majority of firms are still competing across a wide range of segments. In almost every market, firms compete with very little focus across clients, practices and value levels. It is still strongly held that a firm must offer clients a wide range of services in order to be seen as serious. Partners believe that they must be able to say that their firm can do almost everything, even though all of the evidence is that clients select their providers according to the different services they require. Very few clients today (at least with any sophistication) use one firm for all their needs. Until now, most firms have tried to improve the 'full service' concept rather than radically rethink what range of services are needed for future competitiveness. As the chief executive of one major European firm recently said, "Strategic thinking in law firms up to now has been extrapolating from the past – how to make the same business model that we have always had work a bit better. Very few firms have taken a really hard look at where the market is going and adopted a strategic approach that recognises the fundamental change we are facing."

Given our view of the structural changes in the market, firms will need to adopt a different view of their business. They will need to reshape their focus and operate in fewer areas, or at least downgrade some to support activities of smaller size than is current. This alone will mean that partners and other staff will be required to leave or retrain. Clients will feel the same effect. Many firms will need to reduce their number of clients. Our experience is that most law firms, regardless of size, have too many clients either which are unprofitable or which add no strategic value. Often, both are the case. Many are attached to specific partners who refuse to turn them away and thus obstruct efforts to focus on more strategic clients. In addressing the market's structural change, firms offering a fuller service will need to shrink to become more focused and then grow within that narrower focus. Many firms will continue to grow, but will become more defined in focus.

4. Strategic leadership and decision making

The still too strong sense of autonomy in many firms is a serious barrier to a strategic approach. Partners are often unwilling to do what is required to implement a strategy, even if they have expressed agreement with it (or at least not opposed it). Partners repeatedly say that they never refuse new work and new clients (subject to conflict and ethics checks), even if that work might not be profitable and not in line with the firm's agreed strategic focus. There is a very real tendency for partners to assume that any changes that arise from strategy implementation will apply to others and not them. As a consequence, it can be difficult to implement even a moderate strategy. It may be even more difficult to implement a more radical strategy that requires a firm to abandon specific types of work and clients.

Effective strategic leadership is already a critical factor in success and its importance will only increase. A crucial underlying problem in today's law firms is the relationship between partners and the firm's leaders and management. As noted above, partners still assume a high level of autonomy. At one end of the spectrum, they see management as an administrative group, tasked with providing partners with the support they require and letting them get on with their work with as few disturbances as possible. A few firms have made great internal changes in their attitude to management, however. These firms have succesfully transferred considerable power to a leadership group that is able to manage the firm without constant recourse to partners other than in clearly defined, more strategic areas. In these firms the partners accept their dual role as owners and work producers, and realise that under the latter role they need to respect management decisions and not choose to implement only those with which they agree.

If firms wish to be successful, they must clarify how important decisions are made. Firms that do not will be unable to make the tough strategic decisions necessary to address future structural changes. This process must be clarified before making any critical decisions about future market positioning. In too many firms management is able to make and implement only those operational decisions that neither alter the role or status of partners by much nor radically change the overall structure of the firm. Once an issue is likely to affect a partner or group of partners, it is seen as an issue for the partnership as a whole to decide. The problem here is that any issue that has an adverse impact on one group is likely to lead to an impasse. Partners tend to approach issues from a personal and emotional point of view and are often unable to look objectively for what is best for the firm. Fear also plays a part. A decision that has an adverse impact on one group now might be followed by one that has an adverse impact on another. For this reason, partners oppose anything that disturbs the status quo in case their group is next.

Outside crisis situations, many firms' managements have difficulty obtaining consent to any decision that appears negatively to affect one partner or group over another. This issue needs to be addressed as firms restructure themselves so as to compete effectively in the market of the future. Within the ownership and voting systems in place at most firms, the partnership entity can be a major problem when making strategic decisions. Strategic leadership will therefore become a defining issue for success. Some firms will achieve it and benefit, while others will suffer.

This problem has implications in the context of segmentation. The highest-value segment of any market is relatively small and is likely to shrink over time. Services that once commanded high prices become institutionalised as more and more firms become capable in that area. This growth in supply brings down the price and the service is transformed into a mid or low-value one.

In addition, the demands on firms that do occupy the highest-value segment are high. The organisational requirements are expensive, deep expertise and market-leading practitioners are required, and great demands are made on fee earners. These factors restrict the number of firms that can sustain a competitive position. As a consequence, the vast majority of firms will be competing at levels below this segment. Partners need to understand this if they are to make effective strategic choices for the future.

The comments of one managing partner of a large firm illustrate the problem. While not disagreeing with the analysis, he said that no firm at the upper end of a geographical market could afford to say that it was seeking to compete outside the highest-value end of the market. "Partners want to be doing the best work in their market, and we have no choice but to say we are at the very high-value end, or at least striving for it, even if we are not now and unlikely to be there in the future."

Firms need to be able to manage this sort of issue if they are to have any hope of success. Management must be able to develop a future strategic position that is based on the reality of the firm's overall capabilities rather than unrealistic dreams. Failure to do so suggests an absence of strategic leadership. Many of us might have dreamed of winning an Olympic gold medal when we were children. But as adults we realised that the dream was not going to happen and got on with something else in which we could perform well, even if not at gold medal standard. The same is true in business. Taking a realistic view of where a firm will be able to compete and then pursuing this will bring a much greater chance of success than holding out for an impossible strategic position.

A fundamental organisational change is therefore required. If firms are to be able to deal with the structural changes in the market, they must change their decision-making processes. One difficulty is that most partners strongly hold to a partnership ethos, at least when it suits them, and such changes are often seen as an attack on this. The concept of partnership held by many partners is out of line with the current state of the market, let alone that of the future. The view that all partners can decide what they do, how they spend their time and how they operate is not viable in a competitive market. Different firms hold this view in different strengths. But it can be seen in things like the 'my client' syndrome; an unwillingness to engage in activities beyond legal work, such as business development; and an unwillingness to put time into managing staff through performance assessments and the like. In effect, too many partners see themselves as accountable to no one, with the firm simply a supply of resources for the partner to use as he or she desires.

This environment is still not uncommon. But it will need to change dramatically if firms are to survive the structural changes described above. Along with strategic market positioning, this is the second greatest – and equally important – strategic challenge of the future. Organisational changes are not usually seen as strategic challenges, but they are so closely related to the ability to make effective strategic choices that they are, in effect, strategic challenges.

A few firms have gone a long way in tackling this. However, it is important to emphasise that this is not a move to a corporate structure in which management makes all the decisions and partners have no say, but rather a move to an environment that allows difficult choices to be made in a reasonably objective manner.

There are a number of steps to creating a more managed environment in which difficult strategic choices can be made. The first is to understand that the firm is an entity in its own right. Once a firm holds a market position separate from how clients might see individual partners, the rules of engagement alter. While the firm's position and the market's view of it are consequences of the many actions of partners over a number of years, a firm also creates a market image in its own right.

A firm's brand is a promise that clients and prospective clients will consistently receive something of value. A professional firm's brand is largely determined by the behaviour of its partners and other staff. The more uncoordinated they act, the less likely it is that the firm will be able to build a strong brand. If the actions of partners are seen to be out of line with the firm's brand, they can undermine its strategy. Once a firm decides how it wishes to present itself in the market, behaviours that conflict with this can damage its standing. Partners who continue to act as they wish and outside the agreed forms of behaviour can harm the interests of others. Today's business environment therefore requires partners to be accountable to each other.

As with many other activities, accountability exists even if it is not spelled out. A law firm is an organisation like any other. As such, it has to compete against other firms for clients and work. It must do the work well, build strong relationships with strategically important clients, make an appropriate profit, manage people well and manage the internal environment so that people remain committed to the firm and carry out the various activities that are essential for an organisation to operate at a required competitive level. The fact that the ownership entity is a partnership does not change the fact that it has to operate as an effective, efficient and competitive organisation. Failure to do so will result in a loss of competitiveness, with the result that the goals agreed with the owners will not be met. Incomes will likely decrease as a result and the quality of clients and work will be less than desired. When this occurs, the best lawyers start to look for a place that more suits their ambitions. A firm can thus easily enter a downward competitive spiral. A failure by partners to ensure the firm's competitiveness therefore has a negative effect on everyone within the firm.

Equity partners, as the owners of the firm, are responsible for ensuring that the business operates competitively and in the way decided by the owners as a whole. In today's competitive environment it is vital that this be translated into management decisions that can be implemented. The partnership model leads partners into confusion over their dual role. At one level, they are owners with overall responsibility for deciding what is required for the firm's success. On the other hand, they are also producers of output. At the operational level, they have three responsibilities: to assist in implementing the agreed strategy, to manage their part of the business to meet the firm's performance targets and to ensure that the quality of the work performed meets the needs of clients, whether through their own work or through supervision. Many partners see their role only as 'doing legal work' and then oppose, either actively or passively, management decisions directed at implementing a strategy previously agreed by the 'owners'. Whenever a strategy requires a partner to change what he or she has generally been doing, opposition emerges.

As a consequence, partners may take a limited interest in the strategic issues facing the firm until one of three things happens:

- The firm faces a crisis;
- There is a proposal that will change the structure of the firm – either amalgamating groups, abolishing groups or disposing of a group; or
- There is a proposal to change the partnership conditions, such as remuneration, the process for managing partner performance or the removal of underperforming partners.

Put another way, partners tend to exercise their ownership role in direct proportion to the extent that decisions will or may directly affect them. The problem is that any strategic decision to restructure the business in line with market changes will affect some part of the firm, including partners and other staff.

The critical challenge for firms in the future is to be able to take tough strategic decisions even if they appear to be against the interests of a minority. And they must be able to do so before a crisis emerges. Those who achieve this will be able to maintain a competitive position in a changing market. Others might get decisions through, but only after a period of crisis that forces partners to agree to changes that by then will be radical and painful. Others will lose market position and either close down or compete at a much lower value.

Partners will be required to look at what is best for the firm rather than what is best for them or a group of partners. They will need to see the success of their firm as the primary goal and make decisions on that basis rather then their personal feelings about the issues. Equally important will be the ability of management to help individuals and groups who are asked to leave to find new homes where their skills and work focus are needed.

Strategic leadership is therefore of very high importance in a firm. Leaders must be able to assemble a case for restructuring in such a way that no partner can doubt the consequences of failure. As well as describing the type of restructuring required, it will be necessary to assemble both internal and external data to demonstrate market trends. Even then, the leaders' ability to make the case and convince the majority that there is no other solution will be critical. The treatment given to those who will be asked to leave will be key. Before the decision is made, there must be a high degree of consultation and a plan agreed as to how they will be helped to find new roles elsewhere. The high degree of leadership required is one reason why many firms are unable to address this issue before it becomes a crisis. It is common among managers to talk of the need to create a 'burning platform' around issues such as this so as to make it clear that there is a crisis. However, such an issue needs to be addressed even sooner if the firm is to move through this phase quickly. The problem with the 'burning platform' approach is that everyone tries to save what they have. It becomes difficult, as a result, to marshal the majority behind a single strategy. The result is often a period of confusion and disruption, which impedes any progress in building competitiveness.

5.   Aligning economic structures and pricing with strategy

A third, closely related strategic challenge is developing a firm's appropriate economic structure. This was touched on above in relation to the different market positions that a firm might choose. As firms move into strategic positions focused on work that is lower in value and/or more competitive in price than before, they must adjust their economic structure. Achieving an appropriate level of overhead is one aspect of this, but not the most important one. Most critical is the ability of partners to manage work more effectively and so contain costs, as well as to ensure that the firm's overall economic structure and strategy are aligned. This requires a firm's partnership to be able to take tough decisions.

One aspect of economic structure to be tackled is the ratio of equity partners to other fee earners or timekeepers. For a majority of firms today, this ratio is too low, given that most of the work being done is not that complex – at least for a well-trained lawyer. Law is probably the last major profession in which adults aged 45 are still largely doing what they did when they were 25. In most other professions people move into management and development roles as they become more senior, delegating the more technical tasks further down the reporting line. In most firms partners still do too much of the legal work, often on the mistaken assumption that they can do it more cheaply than another fee earner.

The future downward pressure on price for most legal work means that there will be a need for increased leverage. This will change the role of the partner. Partners will need to supervise much more work than they actually do, spend more time on client relationship and business development activities, and create high performance and motivational environments for their teams. This change has already occurred in a few firms, but is not widespread. The exceptions will be genuinely complex work that needs the exceptional skill and experience of a partner. But the vast majority of legal work is not at this level and a partner can do much less than most do today.

Endless surveys suggest that clients want more partner time, and partners often invoke these as a reason for doing more work themselves. However, those surveys also show that clients want that time only when it matters, such as when decisions need to be made or when complex advice has to be communicated. They do not actually want partners to do all the work. One exception to this might be when a client has had poor work from an associate and is led to give an ultimatum. In this case the partner must do the work or the client will move to another firm. This is a result more of bad supervision than of any underlying client requirement. Clients do not always want to pay for the time of associates. But this suggests that they are not seeing the value added to the cost. Either the associates are not adding enough value or they are being too highly paid. The escalation of salaries in the legal profession suggests the latter.

Partners are a firm's most expensive resource. This fact is often hidden because partnerships often fail to record partner costs in their management accounts. In effect, the profit that firms declare is not a profit in a business sense because it does not include the cost of the highest-paid people working in the firm – that is, the partners. If a partnership were to convert to a corporate entity, then the partners would become employees and be paid a salary, even if they remained shareholders of the new entity. In order to resist losing the best to other firms, that salary would have to be competitive. The change in entity makes no difference to the cost: the business has to earn a sum above a competitive amount being paid to its staff before it earns a profit. Partnerships must include a competitive salary figure for partners in their internal accounting (as more are doing) if they are to see that their real profit margins are around 10% and not 30% or higher. Separating the salary component of a partner's income from the profit element is simply good management.

Once real partner costs are calculated, it becomes clear that a vast amount of legal work today cannot include much partner time and still produce an acceptable return to the firm. (This is true even when a partner might be quicker at a task than another fee earner: the difference in time is outweighed by the lower cost of the fee earner.) Partners must therefore create a management or business development role for themselves or they will become a burden. While removing partners who cease to add sufficient value to a firm will improve leverage, it will be some time before it is likely to get a firm to where it needs to be. Another challenge is therefore to determine a firm's correct leverage, given its strategy and the type of work being done. The next step is to decide which partners can perform well in a wider role (and want to) and which cannot. Finally, those who can perform a wider role must be helped to perform at a high level and those who cannot must be helped to find a role elsewhere. This again requires a process of decision making that allows management to manage in the best interests of the firm, rather than of particular individuals. Many partners do not want to do more than legal work. They will need to find a role in other firms where they can, but they will be out of the mainstream.

Following on from this, partners must be able to manage the pricing expectations of clients and manage the cost of the work being processed so that both the agreed price and the required profit are achieved. This reflects the fact that clients now demand greater certainty in pricing and are not prepared to accept open-ended hourly rates. While most firms have for some time applied discount rates and other means of satisfying clients, this is often done on little factual basis. And even when it is, there are overruns of time resulting in even greater cost write-offs. Given the pressure on pricing, it is essential that partners understand the true cost of different types of work and the profit margins required.

Many partners still believe that it is impossible to give a price for an engagement ahead of doing it because each engagement is different. If that is the case, then partners are bringing no experience to their work. If each engagement really is different, then it is as though a partner is starting each one as if it were his or her first. Many are beginning to realise that that is nonsense. Firms need to start looking at historical pricing models, develop staffing templates for work that is done regularly and put in place management processes that allow partners to budget costs and then track them to ensure that the cost is met.

Approaching legal work in this way allows firms to start to look at where efficiencies can be made beyond simply delegating work further down the seniority chain. Many partners still believe that their way of working is superior. As a result, developing standard templates and processes for different work types still meets considerable resistance. Yet studies of work processes indicate a difference in cost of 40% between partners for what is essentially the same work. As in any business, some people are just more efficient than others. Firms that wish to compete outside the very highest-value segments will have no choice but to develop standard processes for almost every work type, allowing for a degree of customisation to meet the variations that can occur. There is real resistance to this, but those firms which succeed in implementing this approach will remain competitive in the face of continuing downward pressure on pricing.

6.   Managing performance at all levels

There are many more challenges than have been referred to here. But the final major challenge that must be mentioned is the management of performance at all levels in a firm, including partner level. Many firms have put in place performance management processes for staff, but there is still resistance from partners to any similar form of assessment for them. Where there is such a process for partners, it often focuses on a very narrow definition of performance – billable hours or revenue.

The arguments made against assessing partner performance are generally spurious or based on bad experiences. It is possible to assess the performance of anyone carrying out an activity, even if this might be more indicative over time than completely accurate at any given moment. The fact that some firms have done this badly is no reason to dismiss any attempt to implement a better system. Partners often argue that the subjective elements of their performance, such as managing a team, cannot be measured. But it is a simple matter to ask the team and look at its output. If output is high and the team is cohesive and motivated, then it is likely that it is being managed effectively.

We noted in the previous section that the role of the partner is moving towards management and business development. As pricing pressure increases, this shift will increase. Partners will come to spend more time on activities other than legal work, and it will be essential to assess performance in all these activities. This is independent of the type of remuneration system in place. Performance assessments are necessary whether the firm is on a lockstep, merit or combined remuneration system. The critical issue is to ensure that all partners are able to meet the required performance standards needed for the firm to achieve its goals. Addressing any issues of sustained underperformance is important, but secondary. The primary purpose of a performance assessment is to help all partners to continually improve their performance; underperformance arises only when some partners are clearly unable to sustain a standard of performance that is within acceptable limits.

What is becoming clear to those who manage law firms is that it is not possible to manage the overall performance of a firm without managing the performance of key individuals who are in charge of those doing the work and the work flow itself. In a competitive environment it is essential that managers be able to influence the performance of everyone in the firm, including the partners. Performance management processes are too often seen as a 'stick' with which to beat those partners who underperform. This perception must change. Performance management processes are there to help partners to perform at the level expected of them.

A clear view of the activities that a partner is expected to carry out is the starting point. As noted above, this will in future be less about personal fee earning and more about the profitability of the work that a partner is managing (note profit, not revenue), alongside business development, client relationship management, team management and other such activities. The next step is to attach a goal to each activity. These will be based broadly on what the firm is seeking to achieve with its strategy. Developing processes to assess each performance will follow from this. This includes both 'hard' and 'soft' measures. The assessment and feedback process must seek to help partners to develop their skills and performance, rather than simply instruct them that they haven't performed – or, even worse, give feedback only to underperforming partners, who are then forced out.

7. Conclusion

The only thing that we can forecast accurately is that the future will not be the same as the past. But the future is nevertheless shaped by past events. So we can still see patterns and trends that suggest some of the issues that are likely to arise.

What is clear from the past, however, is that well-managed businesses are more likely to succeed even in the face of completely unpredictable events. Well-managed businesses are able to adapt more quickly than those that are less well managed, partly because the former are thinking about the future and partly because they have in place the systems and processes that allow them to adapt to new conditions more quickly than others.

The theme of this chapter is the subject of what 'well managed' means for a contemporary law firm. The critical ingredients are:

- effective strategic leadership;
- a clear view about the future competitive positioning of the firm; and
- a viable set of actions for moving the firm towards its long-term goal.

Incorporated within these is the need for a commitment among partners to the strategic position and the action plan. The decision-making process that supports this is also fundamental. We foresee that firms will need to create a greater separation between ownership and control if they are to take some of the difficult decisions required in a more competitive environment. They must also ensure that their operational activities are aligned with the needs of the strategy. This is particularly so when the market is moving towards price competition at almost all levels. This will lead firms to change their business models. This is accompanied by a change in the role of a partner. Around the two is the need to manage the firm's performance; this requires finding ways to help people at all levels to improve their performance.

Of course, many things need to be managed and other changes will be required. One is the greater use of technology to produce legal output in a more efficient way. This will coincide with the need to align a firm's economic structures with its strategic positioning. The need to attract and retain people with an appropriate level of skill is another important issue, although the strategy will determine the type of people and skills. The main role of ensuring that people are motivated to come to and remain with the firm will continue to lie with the partners, but will be lessened by good HR processes.

While we cannot predict the future accurately, we can say that any business that manages the fundamentals well has the chance of a successful future. We have endeavoured in this chapter to demonstrate what those fundamentals are for a law firm in the 21st century.

The impact of the financial crisis

Bryan Hughes
Eversheds LLP

1. Revolution in the legal sector

The global financial crisis has unquestionably had a major impact on the legal sector. Its aftermath has seen a dramatic shift in the balance of power between in-house clients and their external law firm providers. It is arguable whether this change has been a direct result of the credit crisis – there were certainly signs several years ago that the seeds of change had already been sown. But the legal profession is traditionally extremely cautious and hesitant to embrace change of any kind. And the changes experienced over the past two years could be described as seismic. They have caused many within the profession to question the status quo and have almost certainly accelerated attempts on many fronts to keep up with the times.

At Eversheds LLP, we have commissioned two reports into the future shape of the legal profession. These reports were on the subject of the *Law Firm of the 21st Century*, but even we could not have anticipated how timely they would be. The first was produced in 2008, just as the economic downturn was beginning to affect the legal sector. It focused on the likely shape of law firms over the following decade and the changes that were anticipated. The second, published in 2010 as the long-term effects of the downturn were becoming evident, focused on how things had already changed and what the future might hold. This chapter concentrates on the findings of the second report.

The research[1] was based on in-depth interviews with 130 general counsel at top corporate and financial institutions worldwide and interviews with 80 partners at leading international law firms.

Eversheds aims to be the most client-centred international law firm. In order to achieve this, we have invested heavily in researching the needs and expectations of our client base. This has confirmed our view that the legal world has changed and is continuing to change rapidly.

We commissioned these reports to help us to identify what we need to do in order to meet the future demands of the sector. However, these findings are relevant to all parts of the legal sector – large and small firms, and clients from across the spectrum.

2. The shape of the future law firm

So, what is the future of the legal sector? How will the law firm of the future differ

---

1 Carried out on behalf of Eversheds LLP by independent legal research consultancy RSG Consulting Ltd.

from that of the present?

Clients and law firm partners have identified four main themes (in decreasing order of perceived importance) that will transform the legal sector in the future:

- globalisation;
- the increased status of general counsel;
- technology; and
- the Legal Services Act.

The pressure from these four factors during the financial crisis may have created a 'perfect storm' that has precipitated radical change within the sector.

On the basis of these four themes, we have derived a series of attributes that will be vital to any premium law firm wishing to thrive in the 21st century.

2.1 Training lawyers to reflect their clients

Quality will be paramount to the 21st-century law firm; as will the alignment of lawyers with their clients. The top-quality lawyers of the future must be both businesspeople and legal experts. Every good firm will train its lawyers to be commercially minded and to speak the language of its clients.

In the past, most lawyers graduated in law before proceeding through the necessary steps to qualification. Their academic credentials and their ability to cut through legal arguments were impeccable, but they often lacked any understanding of economics or business. In the years before the economic downturn, firms were developing a sectoral approach, in tandem with the old approach of practice areas. In many cases this was more cosmetic than substantial and few firms had genuine experts in each sector.

Increasing numbers of firms, including our own, have introduced MBA modules into their training. This trend is likely to continue. The emphasis for new talent is likely to shift from academic prowess to commercial experience. Mature entrants with industry and business experience may be increasingly in demand. In recognition that legal teams should reflect their clients in more than just commercial understanding, law firms are already increasing access to those from non-traditional and underprivileged backgrounds.

The overriding theme of the interviews with general counsel was that their legal advisers must develop a more symbiotic partnership in which each has the best interests of the other at heart. This may mean blurring the lines between the internal and external legal teams. Each can complement the other, with the best external legal teams working to enhance the status of the internal team within their organisations. This is in marked contrast to the former system, in which external legal providers were a constant financial drain. Now that general counsel are more confident in their buying power and influence, they can command increased respect from their legal advisers. The canny firm will use a close relationship with its clients to enhance its own business model and develop new business lines that it can sell to a receptive in-house counsel.

2.2 Cutting down the flab

The law firm of the future will be lean and streamlined. During the recession, many firms began to cut down the 'flabbiness' that was endemic in the early, happier years of the millennium. It seems likely that this trend towards a leaner model will persist even as firms are beginning to see their profit-per-partner figures increase once more. By the time of the economic downturn, law firms had become like unwieldy ships – hard to manoeuvre and extremely slow to turn. The fee-earning core staff of the modern firm, who carry out legal services that require legal training and expertise, had become a small minority.

After the recession and into the future, law firms will refocus on their key attributes: their lawyers. Support staff can be outsourced. Certain tasks can be commoditised and handled in low cost centres. The firm will then directly provide the resources for that work that is of high value to the client and demands high-quality legal expertise.

Our research also found the trend towards leanness within the ranks of legally qualified staff. Specialist lawyers, who had narrow experience and at the time of the credit crisis were working in silos, had no role when their specialist market collapsed. The increasing significance of general counsel has renewed the view that overspecialisation does not reflect the needs of clients. In-house counsel must view all elements of their legal work as interconnected. They therefore need joined-up thinking from their legal advisers, not a series of experts working in isolation.

Technology enhances and complements a firm's high-quality offering. The past few years have seen the legal profession realise the extent to which technological innovation might benefit its clients and its own business. Project management tools, the standardisation of legal and non-legal processes, the use of new media to communicate with and educate clients – now that the profession has opened its mind, the possibilities are endless. The use of technology to promote remote working and instant communication, as well as to facilitate the 24-hour servicing of clients across time zones and across continents, is set to continue to increase the process of globalisation.

2.3 Looking to the East

Many firms are turning their sights East. A significant number have had Hong Kong offices since the days when British rule made it an obvious gateway, but the international legal elite is being attracted to other Eastern outposts as well. The rise of India and China as economic powerhouses and sources of low-cost manpower make them attractive to all businesses, and the legal sector is no exception. However, law firms face a particular challenge in certain jurisdictions, such as India, where protectionism has long precluded them from practising. This is forcing the sector to be creative. International firms are vying to form relationships with local firms, training their own Indian lawyers and doing what they can to service UK companies based in India from 'offshore' hubs such as Singapore.

As firms expand their offices in Asia and the Middle East, they will slim down their expensive European and North American bases. We anticipate that those firms currently headquartered in the United Kingdom and the United States will ultimately move their headquarters to the East.

2.4　The shape of the future law firm

Following our research, we believe that the legal profession will change greatly over the next few years. As the world emerges slowly from the recession, the market for premium legal services will continue to shrink. Our respondents expect there to be a tight elite of truly globalised premium law firms, followed by a new competitive order and categorisation.

Even the dominant firms will tend to be smaller and better hedged against future threats. They will consist of more generalist, business-qualified lawyers arranged according to where premium-quality work is available. They will be structured for maximum efficiency, maximum value and maximum quality. Support services will mainly be outsourced. Some will be sent offshore. Firms are set to become more partner heavy, with an anticipated ratio of 1:2. Lawyers will be more general in ability and able to turn their hands to various disciplines within industry specialisms. Some of the major service providers may not be partnerships, but will have remodelled themselves in the wake of the Legal Services Act. The fees of the boom years, based on hourly rates, will be a thing of the past. Clients will demand genuine value through lower fee levels and a mix of fixed fees and value billing. Fewer types of work will continue to attract an hourly rate.

3.　Key drivers

The second *Law Firm of the 21st Century* report found that the financial crisis had not in itself been a major driver for change within the legal profession. However, it had accelerated the effect of pre-existing factors. Some managing partners felt that the recession may have brought these effects forward by as much as a decade.

Both partners and clients felt that the factors most likely to change the profession were:

- the changing role of general counsel;
- globalisation;
- technology; and
- the Legal Services Act in the United Kingdom.

3.1　The changing role of general counsel

In-house counsel have found themselves in an increasingly unenviable position. On the one hand, boards have traditionally viewed them as a cost centre, accountable for both annual legal fees and any potential negative publicity arising from legal actions against their organisation. On the other, they are at the mercy of large law firms, which charge hourly rates with very little accountability when costs spiral out of control. Viewed as the poor relation of the private practice lawyer, their status within the legal sector and the management structure of their own organisations was relatively low.

Thing were already beginning to change before the recession. In 2008's *Law Firm of the 21st Century* report, it was seen that clients were beginning to chafe at the indiscriminate use of hourly fees. They were seen as unsustainable. Clients felt that firms needed to align themselves more to their businesses.[2] The credit crisis has

---

2　　　Fifty three per cent of clients interviewed.

added momentum to this trend: over-regulation has had an effect and the remit of the in-house lawyer has broadened. As in-house counsel are increasingly seen as strategic partners within the business and vital to its success an opportunity has arisen for external counsel to support and enhance in-house counsel's role.

3.2 Globalisation

The legal trade press is full of stories of international law firms opening ever more offices around the world. It is hardly a surprise, therefore, that even 12 months ago our interviewees regarded globalisation as the most significant influence on the future law firm.[3] While we anticipate that the future holds room for no more than a handful of truly global firms, the other effects of globalisation will be more widespread. As clients become increasingly globalised, their need for seamless cross-jurisdictional expertise ensures that internationalisation will continue.

3.3 Technology

Unsurprisingly, clients were further ahead in their use of technology in their businesses than law firms. However, it was a surprise that just over one-third of the managing partners of the top firms said that they were actively investing in technology, to standardise legal processes, to communicate more effectively or both.

3.4 The Legal Services Act

The likely effect of this UK legislation on premium and global law firms is still unclear. However, between 2008 and 2010 there was a shift away from blanket dismissal of the Legal Services Act as irrelevant. General counsel appeared to welcome the act, believing it would bring them a better buying position. Our respondents anticipated a change in the structure of premium law firms, switching emphasis from the outmoded partnership structure to that of a service provider. However, most firms will probably stick to the tried and tested formula.

Perhaps the act's greatest impact will be through its rewriting of traditional rules, presenting an atmosphere of change to the profession as a whole. The mere potential for change can actually drive change. However, only a small minority[4] of respondents saw the Legal Services Act as having a transformative effect on the legal sector of the future.

4. Conclusion

For many years, our approach at Eversheds has been to view the world through the eyes of our clients. A commitment to client service is one of the pillars of our strategy. The findings of the 2010 *Law Firm of the 21st Century* report confirmed some of the themes we had already sensed from our clients. Our emphasis has long been on collaboration and partnership with clients across the many jurisdictions in which we work. This has helped us emerge as one of the most innovative international law firms and one of the most client centred.

---

3   Thirty seven per cent of all respondents.
4   Eight per cent of all respondents.

What is evident is that many organisations are demanding more from their in-house counsel. The proliferation of regulation and sanctions for non-compliance has pushed general counsel into a position of unprecedented status. This new pivotal role has also given them greater power in their relationship with external counsel. But this higher profile brings increased expectations. Today's in-house counsel are expected to keep a tight control over costs, while ensuring minimal exposure to risk and maintaining the highest quality of outputs.

The new-look professional general counsel are now at the heart of changes within the industry. They will increasingly find themselves on the board and must bring the rest of their team into this increasingly high-profile position. This means a change in culture and no doubt a streamlining and reappraisal of internal resources. With all the competing calls on time and energy, the new general counsel will need considerable support just to keep on course, let alone to bring about the radical changes that are needed in the post-recession climate.

In order to support general counsel, in-house teams should be equipped with the tools to boost their internal status and profile while keeping their external law firms in line. At Eversheds, we do this through project management tools that allow counsel total cost control and transparency on transactions and cases across every jurisdiction in which they operate, through focused training in key performance indicators, through selling in our own management consultancy service and so on. Above all, we have made it our business to understand the needs of in-house counsel and to grow with them. Our commitment to innovation testifies to our thirst for self-improvement and for devising and implementing pioneering ways to run our business and serve our clients. Technology has long been important to developing our offering to clients. For many years we have used technology to help us refine legal processes and push costs down for our clients. And our groundbreaking partnership with Accenture has helped us to streamline our business while ensuring that we have the truly global footprint that our clients need.

Case study 1: Innovating to stay ahead of the game
The legal landscape is constantly changing. In the aftermath of the credit crunch, and with the Legal Services Act set to open up the market, this has never been more true. The way clients want to pay is changing. The way clients want services delivered is changing. And although the ability to innovate and change has long differentiated Eversheds, the firm is keen not to become complacent.

In an increasingly competitive market, Eversheds is committed to constantly improving the service it provides. The firm has long been seen as forward thinking and has been recognised for embracing revolutionary new ideas. It has put infrastructure in place to encourage and capture innovations and ensure that strong ideas are implemented.

The firm has an Innovation Group. This is a senior management committee that sets the firm's strategy and innovation agenda. It has been tasked with investigating how the firm can maximise its opportunities to win new business and best meet the needs of its clients. Its plan is to promote innovation across the firm through awards, the development of IT platforms and practice-based projects aimed at improving profitability and client service.

The firm's practice group champions disseminate the innovation strategy and gather ideas. An online discussion forum, the Innovation Forum, is provided on the firm's intranet. It is open to anyone within the firm as a way to propose ideas and present them to management. Innovation awards are given every month and there is a substantial annual prize for the best overall idea.

The majority of innovations across the firm depend upon a strong IT platform. The continued investment in and development of new IT platforms help the firm to stay ahead of the competition. Regular communication with staff ensures that innovation is kept at the front of everybody's mind.

Innovation is at the core of the firm's strategy and at the heart of its internal operations, client approach and future growth plans. The firm's management views it as a key factor in the firm's future success. The management is dedicated to constant self-improvement and to pushing staff constantly to adapt and change.

The innovation project is a democratic tool designed to empower everyone in the firm. It presents those who might normally feel excluded from decision-making processes with an opportunity to contribute directly to the firm's bottom line. The forum and awards are open to all legal and non-legal staff, from the most junior employees to heads of department and the senior management team. This level of inclusivity has helped to engender a culture in which innovation is part of the firm's DNA.

It is easy to reward a good idea, but not so easy to make it happen. The innovation group at Eversheds is committed to pursuing ideas at every level. It works hard to ensure that everyone with a good idea is involved in its implementation. These people are excused some of their usual duties to dedicate time to doing so.

Case study 2: Empowering general counsel – the key to law firm growth

In recognition of the fact that the law firm of today looks drastically different from that of two, let alone 10 years ago, Eversheds has made a series of fundamental changes to the services it offers.

The firm is committed to listening to the needs of general counsel, seeing them as key to its future growth. In order to to provide general counsel with the advice they need, the firm has developed Eversheds Consulting.

This is a standalone legal consultancy offered to in-house legal teams. It provides advice on how to manage their legal responsibilities more efficiently. A mix of consultants and highly experienced lawyers work with multinational clients to ensure that in-house legal teams are more effective and better able to manage their legal responsibilities and hold their own within the business. It is a pioneering project, the outcome of years of experience in large-scale project management and smart resourcing, and the development of a service ethos with demanding international clients.

Eversheds Consulting provides the modern in-house counsel with the skills to run and manage the legal function and manage relationships with external legal providers. It also provides them with the tools to manage their own reputation within the firm. That is, it provides all of the necessary skills except legal expertise itself. Post-credit crisis and post-Legal Services Act, it is the logical next step for legal businesses.

General counsel at leading organisations should not be seen as a drain on resources. Instead, when they are proactive and savvy, they can add measurable value, deliver greater efficiency and even generate profit for their businesses. Eversheds has taken care to orientate its business and its legal services towards general counsel, particularly those at large multinationals. Its multi-jurisdictional offering and its focus on measurement, predictability and accountability are geared towards such clients, and it has seen notable success as a result.

The firm spent years honing its skills through innovative and progressive partnerships with large multinational clients such as DuPont, Tyco and FMC. In doing so, it learnt through trial and error what project-management systems were needed to manage large-scale projects and how to coordinate and track many-sided management issues.

In some respects Eversheds Consulting grew organically out of a realisation that the firm could also sell its non-legal expertise. It has learnt to be highly competitive on price and resourcing without compromising its own profit margin. For this reason it was among the first to offer its clients alternative pricing structures and creative cash-flow solutions during the recession.

Case study 3: Putting client service excellence at the heart of online legal offerings

The Eversheds Client Console is the first of the next generation of online legal services. It gives clients increased power and flexibility by allowing them to see the online availability of their fee earners. They can chat with them in real time through web and mobile devices. Financial information, including current and historic legal spend, is available at the touch of button. Through the online dashboard, clients can prioritise the information that matters most to them.

The client console represents a major innovation within the legal marketplace. Its innovative approach includes:

- cost transparency;
- fee earner accessibility; and
- geographic flexibility.

All clients want cost transparency. The client console makes past and current financial information available via the Web and mobile devices. Invoices can be broken down, viewed as PDF or Excel files and easily queried to ensure that there are no hidden surprises. By these means, general counsel are given exceptional power and the ability to analyse their legal costs in a flexible and convenient way.

In a world in which emails dominate and telephone calls are not always possible, staying in touch with fee earners can be difficult. The Eversheds Client Console represents a third way. By using instant messaging technology, the firm has been able to integrate real-time text chat into its online services. This is the perfect solution for those quick messages that do not warrant a telephone call, but that are too important to be lost in someone's inbox.

Sometimes, however, a call is needed. A colour-coded traffic light system is used to show a fee earner's availability, and makes it easier to know when to pick up the phone.

Many clients need to be geographically flexible. Eversheds believes that access to key financial information and the ability to connect instantly with senior fee earners will make the lives of general counsel easier. The client console aims to achieve this. Allowing access to document assembly services and deal rooms via the Web or mobile devices provides both power and flexibility on the go.

Eversheds aims to empower its clients not only to manage their legal matters effectively, but also to develop commercial advantages over their competitors, wherever they may be located. In an increasingly globalised, digitised and 24/7 culture, access to powerful online services is not only essential; it can also be the key to a competitive advantage.

The Eversheds Client Console tackles each of these distinct challenges. Its unique solutions make the lives of busy in-house counsel easier. In this way, excellence in client service is placed first and foremost.

Case study 4: Aligning the firm with its clients' businesses

Eversheds has joined with Accenture to improve the firm's finance, procurement and HR services. This partnership has already seen HR administration and accounting departments outsourced, and the relationship continues to develop.

A key reason for partnering with Accenture was to use its global presence to meet the needs of Eversheds' international clients and provide consistent client service across all territories.

Eversheds has over 40 offices around the world. Many of its clients are large multinationals who are looking for a seamless service across all jurisdictions in which they operate. Eversheds' partnership with Accenture allows the firm to standardise its processes internationally and better reflect the structure and integration levels of its clients.

Under this agreement, discrete elements of the firm's support functions have already been sent offshore. Outsourcing has in recent years become a growing trend in the legal sector, but sending offshore is still relatively new and untested ground.

The purpose of sending some of the HR and financial services offshore was to:

- use Accenture's entensive expertise in procurement, finance and administration, and HR processes to deliver a better service to Eversheds' clients and identify opportunities for streamlining;
- focus in-house HR and finance departments on delivering client service. Transferring the finance operations to Accenture has allowed in-house

teams to focus on building their business partnering model;

- reduce operational overheads;
- innovate in the future. A strong partnership between Eversheds and Accenture has provided opportunities for meeting client needs better and streamlining the processing of transactions;
- use technology to provide the business with timely and accurate information; and
- improve the security of Eversheds' information and data.

The relationship with Accenture has maximised efficiencies. But its primary motivation has been to optimise client services. Both organisations saw this as an opportunity to set an industry benchmark and both view it as a chance to pursue further innovative solutions.

Bigger isn't always better

Charles Martin
Macfarlanes LLP

1. Introduction

Any consideration of law firm strategy should begin with what clients want now and what they are likely to want in the future. Many firms once had the luxury of running themselves and their practices in whatever way they wanted and of offering their services similarly. And to a considerable degree, clients tolerated that. Now firms know that they do not exist in a vacuum. They can be sustained only if they meet a particular market need. If, for example, the market wants only large law firms, then that is the only size of firm that will succeed.

Clients come in all shapes and sizes, with needs ranging from the highly complex and business critical to the mundane and administrative. Some operate within narrowly defined local markets, others on a global scale. Some clients have sophisticated legal functions of their own, others have none. Some clients want their lawyers to provide advice and counsel, others simply want their clear instructions to be executed efficiently.

Lawyers have widely varying skill sets, ambitions and financial expectations. All can be expected, from their professional qualification and continuing education, to have a core competence of intelligence and basic legal knowledge. Beyond that, however, their personal qualities will range from a deep understanding of people through business talents to a focus on technical legal issues. Some individuals will therefore concentrate on understanding a client's business, adding value through providing bespoke advice. Others will provide a broader range of more day-to-day process management services, in which efficiency and effective execution are to the fore. Some lawyers are happiest addressing complex and technical legal issues without client distractions.

Many of the most talented and ambitious lawyers bring a highly questioning and independent approach to their work. They may well be reluctant or unable to function in a team or in an environment where they are subject to the strictures of management. However, it is difficult for large firms to operate efficiently if key partners do not operate as part of a team and accept necessary or desirable constraints.[1]

For these reasons, one type or size of law firm will never fit all client needs and will never be able to attract, retain or motivate an appropriate range of lawyers to service all those needs. In today's legal market, different types and sizes of firms co-

---

[1]   See, for example "Aligning the Stars: How to Succeed when Professionals Drive Results" by Lorsch and Tierney for an in-depth analysis of these issues.

exist. They will continue to thrive, provided that they are clear about what they offer clients. In an increasingly crowded legal marketplace, scale is rarely key to delivering excellent service. It is more important to be the right firm for the client and the job, offering clear client benefits and achieving excellence within your firm's category, whether it be global, international, niche or boutique. Indeed, there may be more similarities (in terms of quality of people, clients and work) between the very top performers across different categories of firm than between those firms and less successful firms in the same category. Bigger isn't always better.

2. Scale: perceived advantages

But what about the other side of the story? What are the benefits of size? When do these benefits mean that bigger is better? And how can smaller firms compete in the face of those benefits?

2.1 Global reach

Scale is clearly necessary for a firm to offer true global reach. In theory, it might be possible in a narrow field for a small firm to offer a global service, but in practice there are few good examples of this. The closest example may be Bird & Bird in IT/telecoms. Global reach offers clients with global needs a one-stop shop for their requirements.

A smaller firm needs to interrogate client needs more deeply to find out how it can compete successfully. As the general counsel of a FTSE 100 company, nearly all of the cross-border requirements of his organisation are "point to point", rather than global as such. In that regard, law is very different from accountancy, particularly on the audit side or indeed management consultancy, where global standards apply and global coverage is essential when servicing large clients. A particular contract or transaction might have legal implications in two or three jurisdictions, but rarely more. Exceptions include certain HR issues, categories of regulatory advice, IP protection and financial transactions involving multinational companies.

Well-run smaller firms can keep overheads and administrative costs down. The management challenges and costs of running a single large law firm that can consistently deliver global reach are not to be underestimated. Whether those costs, once passed on to the client, make for better value than operating through several independent firms is uncertain. However, they will for some clients for some of their needs.

Clients have different cost expectations in different markets. Firms based in the relevant market can readily respond to these. One impact of the growth in global law firms has been the introduction of more uniform charging structures for clients across their networks. This has, for the most part, been achieved by introducing structures that approximate those of the most expensive business centres (notably London and New York) into jurisdictions that have historically seen lawyers charge in different ways and/or at lower rates. Germany is a good example of this. There, high-quality independent firms charge both domestic and international clients at rates that reflect the lower costs of doing business there without the need to pass on the costs of delivering global reach. Similar examples may be found in many other jurisdictions. Incidentally, the uniform rate model is struggling, particularly in Asia.

Smaller firms can be more flexible and opportunistic about the clients that they serve. Global firms rightly want to serve clients with global needs. Many therefore discourage partners in individual jurisdictions from taking on domestic clients, however prestigious or valuable. The concern is that those clients may divert resources away from strategically important global clients, may not be prepared to pay the premium rate that a global platform commands and may create conflicts of interest that might prevent the firm from acting for a global client, thereby upsetting that client and potentially allowing a competitor to intervene.

Lawyers who hope to build a practice, possibly becoming closely trusted advisers to their clients in the process, might well find such a proposition hard to accept. In the Paris market, a number of lawyers have migrated from global firms to French firms in search of the freedom to build their domestic client base. In the Italian market, many law firms have found the degree of central management and control demanded of the global model not to their liking. Some lawyers might, of course, find the possibility of being a partner in a firm that is more profitable than all but a very few leading domestic firms irresistible. Or they might find the scale and complexity of work that global firms target or the lustre of a global brand name simply irresistible. But not all will, by any means.

Global reach is not, of course, the exclusive preserve of global firms. While it is undeniable that the global business firm model is currently popular (eg, Hogan Lovells, Norton Rose), independent firms can often deliver a superior global service. Many more sophisticated clients do not see global reach as necessary, at least for their high-end, complex work.

The difficulty for independent firms is convincing clients that they can provide a truly integrated, reliable and consistent service. This means investing heavily in building relationships between firms over a number of years so that the client has total comfort that it will not be disadvantaged by dealing with multiple organisations. This may be through secondments or compatibility of IT systems (eg, not only in the areas of document production, but also in billing and the delivery of intranets and like). These firms are also required to work with each other in the spirit of partnership. In other words, the objective is to enhance the relationship between the client and the firm initially instructed by the client. Sharp elbows or jockeying for position will destroy a client's confidence in this way of working. The firm that commands the client relationship must also ensure that the overall arrangement is efficiently coordinated, and that advice is properly communicated and understood. In other words, there must be a considerable degree of mutual reliance.

A major advantage of this model is that top-level expertise can be tapped, particularly in more specialist areas such as tax or competition law, in a way that global firms may struggle to match consistently across their networks.

2.2 Economies of scale

Certain aspects of running a modern law firm can be centralised and deployed across multiple offices. These economies of scale might benefit the firm, its clients or both. Moving marketing, financial administration, secretarial services or paralegal support to low-cost locations would be examples of this.

Information technology is helping small organisations to reap many economies of scale. For example, legal process outsourcing is now available to almost any law firm. This may enable a small independent firm operating in a high-cost jurisdiction to outsource elements of its administration or legal process to a low-cost jurisdiction through a third-party provider. In this way, some of the benefits of scale can be achieved without some of the disadvantages.

The number of areas in which economies of scale may apply within law firms are quite limited. Most law firms' costs increase in direct proportion to lawyer headcount, making economies of scale hard to achieve. In law firm mergers, synergies are often presented as benefits of scale, but in reality they are often cost savings that might be achievable without a merger but which, politically and presentationally, are achievable only if wrapped up as part of the merger.

2.3   Breadth of service offering

A large law firm can offer depth in a wide variety of legal specialities that a smaller firm cannot do. A larger firm will also be more likely to have seen a problem or issue before and be able to produce a solution.

Not all large firms are full service, by any means. Indeed, many of the world's most successful and profitable law firms confine themselves to relatively narrow categories of corporate, regulatory and contentious work. Those that aim to be full service, at least for corporate clients with a global footprint, rarely offer a consistently high-quality service across all practice areas and in all jurisdictions. Sophisticated clients may therefore supplement the weaker elements of a large firm with focused advice from more specialist firms. For example, the competition law aspects of a transaction may be handled by a different firm from that handling the corporate or financing aspects. Macfarlanes, as a case in point, is asked to deal with the tax or pensions aspects of transactions or financings to boost the capability of firms that are considered weaker in those areas.

Online research databases have helped to shrink the knowledge gap between large and small firms. The information provided by the likes of PLC and LexisNexis means that the knowledge that was once the preserve of the elite firms is readily accessible by all. Indeed, a strong argument for retaining the split legal profession in the United Kingdom (in other words, a separate and independent bar, offering access to barristers with deep specialist expertise) is that it gives clients greater choice in accessing specialist legal expertise.

I do not want to suggest that large firms focusing on high-end work do not have a great many excellent lawyers in them. Indeed, in absolute numerical terms those firms almost certainly have more outstanding lawyers than can be found at smaller firms. Larger firms will have an undoubted competitive advantage for clients which are looking for a firm that can offer multiple teams of outstanding lawyers (eg, when a conglomerate is looking to dispose of and acquire many businesses at the same time). For that reason, larger firms undertook much of the work for governments at the time of the global financial crisis. However, such situations and needs are relatively infrequent.

2.4 Depth of resources

Some legal needs call for large numbers of lawyers to be available at relatively short notice. Only large firms can carry that capacity.

The categories of work of which this is true are quite small in number. Obvious examples are large-scale litigation, large and complex corporate transactions on tight timetables and extensive forensic reports. These undeniably important categories of work are handled well by a large firm, even if smaller firms can handle substantial aspects of them. This fact has helped to drive global law firm growth.

However, the increasing availability of pools of high-quality contract lawyers and paralegals, as well as those third-party legal processing providers mentioned above, has changed this. Large-scale work can often be carried out effectively by a smaller firm, possibly with a higher degree of relevant specialist expertise, tapping the necessary resources through outsourcing. Indeed, many clients want larger firms to use this type of resource for cost reasons. Macfarlanes has used this model successfully to take on defence work in mass tort litigation where large amounts of evidence and multiple claims have to be handled efficiently and on short time scales.

2.5 Profile

A number of elements make up a firm's profile. Large firms will do more work and therefore rank more highly in league tables and the like. They will win further work based on this profile and reputation, creating a virtuous circle. They will also be able to justify larger aggregate marketing budgets (even if the spend per lawyer is no greater than at smaller firms), thereby getting still more attention. All of this improves the firm's goodwill, allowing it to attract more clients and, possibly, charge more for its services.

Legal services at the higher-value end of the market are not homogeneous. Many clients are too sophisticated to be led by the superficial allure of size or profile alone. Instead, they will look at the substance, quality and value of the service being provided. Again, information technology and the ability to look behind the brand and at the substance of what a firm offers enable clients to make smart choices.

2.6 Career progression

If larger firms can offer talented lawyers a more attractive career path (historically code for a better chance of becoming a partner), then they will win talent at the expense of smaller firms.

Career prospects are not a function of scale as such, as many lawyers found to their cost at the time of the global financial crisis. In a number of cases, it was the larger, more managed firms that made the first redundancies.

A larger organisation will, in theory, offer an excellent young lawyer a broader range of career options. However, that advantage might be short lived, given the increasing tendency for lawyers to specialise early in their career and the difficulty of switching to a different area as their careers progress.

Furthermore, real career prospects have more to do with technical or client skills, combined with the rate of growth of the firm, than the absolute scale of the organisation of which the individual is a part.

3.   Other key considerations

So far, I have examined the widely perceived advantages of scale. Now I look at some other aspects of law firm organisation and consider the relative advantages of scale in these areas.

3.1   Interrelationship between size and management structures

Scale has eroded the partnership ethos in all but a relatively small number of large firms. Although this has freed partners to focus on client relationships without the pressures of management, it has also changed the character of law firms. This in turn has affected the service that clients receive – positively in some ways, but negatively in others.

One reason for this is a declining sense of ownership. Some large firms have sought to recognise this through the introduction of special committees that represent partners as owners separately from those committees that are charged with the management of the firm.

Partnership in the traditional sense (and in the sense that is still found in a few large and many smaller firms) offers a number of advantages. It reflects the high levels of personal autonomy that lawyers have historically expected.

Ownership in a meaningful sense (particularly in a partnership structure that imposes joint and several liability among partners) is an effective and informal governance tool. Collective decision making may lead to a greater consistency of style and standards than a governance model that seeks to impose them.

This is not to say that those who manage large firms cannot take steps to preserve the partnership ethos in their firm, whatever its scale or governance structure. But it is clearly difficult to achieve. And having a consensual, consultative governance structure is not without its disadvantages. Important decisions can take a long time to work through and the opportunity cost of having partners engaged in them is considerable. The cultural benefits must justify the drawbacks.

3.2   Motivation and performance

Much academic work has examined professionals' expectations of high levels of personal autonomy and the problems that arise when they do not get it.[2] Yet professionals are motivated by many other factors, including the wish to establish a strong personal reputation. Not all large firms cater well for this. Some emphasise management and other 'firm' activities over client work. Indeed, an interesting cultural distinction between large UK-based and large US-based law firms is that US firms tend to impose fewer management tasks on their partners, freeing them to focus on clients.

This need for autonomy is one of the reasons why professionals need intellectually rewarding work. They may find this at high-quality law firms in all categories. However, larger firms that focus principally on the financial, business and management aspects of the practice may fail to deliver. For that reason professional services firms have historically been structured as partnerships. This structure is not

---

2   See, for example, *Managing the Modern Law Firm*, edited by Laura Empson, Chapter 2: "Your Partnership".

only a convenient legal framework, but it also imports a number of cultural and control mechanisms that satisfy these fundamental needs.

In order for autonomy not to disintegrate into anarchy, and for the overall alignment of partners with the firm's standards, culture and strategy to be retained, there needs to be a degree of formal or informal accountability between partners. Clearly established norms of behaviour are required, as well as an expectation that partners will be accountable to the firm and the partnership for any shortcomings.[3]

3.3   Communication styles and culture

How a firm operates will significantly affect the service that it delivers. Large firms often need to adopt a corporate internal communication style, at least at the firm level. A greater degree of informality may, of course, operate at the level of the office or practice group. But this gives rise to a danger of creating sub-cultures and sub-loyalties (to the local office or the practice group), rather than to the firm as a whole. Law firm cultures need to be relevant and need to evolve, but a firm's fundamental values and approach will have a considerable effect on all aspects of its practice. This is because those who fit with the culture will be attracted to it and tend to remain, and those who do not will move on or not join in the first place. That leads to a differentiation in the firm's personality and the way in which its service is delivered to its clients. It is clearly more of a challenge to identify, develop and maintain a clear set of values and culture in a larger firm. Geographical diversity adds to the challenge.

3.4   Service integration

Complex client work almost invariably involves teamwork across disciplines. The same is true for business development activities. In both of these areas, partners need to be given incentives, through internal disciplines or by the consistent adoption of clear cultural norms of behaviour, to work with each other for mutual benefit. (Appropriately structured reward mechanisms can also play a part, and I refer to these below.) A firm that fails to deliver this may not realise the potential of its client base and may also disappoint clients. Clearly, a large firm can use information technology to ensure that partners across its network are able to share information and cooperate on both client work and business development. In an age of information overload, the informal communication and genuine personal relationships that are naturally fostered in smaller firms will often be more effective.

3.5   Mentoring and development

Fostering an environment in which partners feel motivated to mentor juniors for the benefit of the firm and the practice in the long term is an essential component for the longer-term success of a law firm. Again, the choices for delivering this are either organisational or cultural. The old master/apprentice model used to be the most effective. In that model the master either handed on his or her practice in due course, or the apprentice left and set up with an apprentice of his own. One of the principal

---

3   See *True Professionalism* by Maister, Chapter 9: "The Value of Intolerance".

engines behind law firm growth is a fundamental rejection of that model. In other words, there is now a wish to ensure that the apprentice stays and the best are offered partnership. Unless this is coupled with considerable management discipline to move people on at the right time, that model results in almost inevitable growth. The decoupling of the master/apprentice relationship and the breakdown of loyalties created is a problem for all growing firms.

3.6 Partner compensation structures

Creating partner compensation structures that work in multiple jurisdictions with different market characteristics is particularly difficult. The subtle balance between structures that encourage positive teamwork (eg, cross-marketing and working across disciplines) and motivate individuals to excel can be disturbed by wide cultural variances. Some global firms satisfy themselves with operating under a global umbrella – for example, a Swiss *Verein*. These can give a great deal of flexibility, but may create only a limited global profit pool. The price of flexibility is the loss of the potential for alignment offered by a structure that encourages all partners around the world to see the firm as a whole thrive, rather than merely their corner of it.

Top New York and London firms find it hard to apply their lock-step compensation systems globally. For this reason, some have created two-tier partnerships, with local partners who are not equity partners. Others have lost partners to firms which are not so constrained. A lock-step system can work successfully only if quality thresholds for admitting and retaining partners are rigorously applied and their contribution is closely monitored to make sure that it falls within a relatively narrow spectrum. All of this sits uneasily with the more pragmatic, flexible approach that is often called for when dealing with local market conditions across the world.

3.7 Growth

I have left this key and difficult subject until last. A managing partner at another firm once remarked to me that "growth is the easy bit – it's what happens when you take your eye off the ball". That may be something of an overstatement. Yet there is some truth in his comment. Supporting growth is not easy. A law firm, particularly in more straitened economic times, grows from the bottom up. To control this, it requires rigorous control of the quality and contribution of lawyers. A hard-nosed approach to what clients and work to take on at all levels is also required if the profitability of the business is not to be diluted. This is not to say that all firms that have grown, even those that have grown rapidly, have necessarily done so at the expense of this rigour. But as a generalisation, it is clearly easier to be disciplined if growth is not an objective in itself.

Whether and how to grow is a key strategic decision that firms must make for themselves. Deciding not to grow is not without its own risks in a world in which many see the benefits of scale as overwhelming. Some firms also believe that their reputations will be enhanced by increased revenues and headcounts, even if this comes at the expense of weaker overall financial performance.

4. The future

In a limited number of areas, larger high-quality firms have advantages over smaller firms of similar quality. By the same token, larger firms face serious challenges in some areas where smaller firms enjoy distinct advantages. A smaller firm is, in many ways, better equipped to deal with many of the internal issues with which larger firms struggle. They can present an excellent service to clients, some of which value this more than the undoubted benefits of larger firms.

Many changes in the market will allow smaller firms to build on their advantages. Information technology allows larger firms to achieve a high level of formal service integration, for example. But smaller firms can be just as effective by relying more on personal relationships and informal communication.

The legal market is becoming increasingly complex. While consolidation (and therefore the creation of ever-larger firms) is undoubtedly a trend, differentiation is increasingly evident among successful independent firms. Highly focused boutiques are springing up as partners leave larger firms. The ease with which clients can use information technology to identify the most suitable firm for a job is accelerating this process.

Despite some consolidation, the legal services market remains hugely fragmented. This reflects both the variety of client expectations and practising lawyers' aspirations. There are fewer market drivers that will force consolidation – unlike the audit needs of global companies that have forced consolidation in the accounting world, for example.

It is always dangerous to offer a view on how things will look at a particular point in the future. But looking 10 years ahead, it is reasonable to suppose that the stars in the legal firmament will be aligned in a different way. There will be a small number (say, half a dozen) of genuinely elite global law firms, a similar number of international business law firms, a small number of high-quality smaller firms with distinctive client offerings, focused boutique players and national firms mostly doing commoditised work. In the United Kingdom that last category will be affected by the Legal Services Act. It may well be that these firms will not be law firms at all, or at least will not be controlled by lawyers.

Only time will tell whether this vision proves correct. But until then, I hope that the reader will agree that although there is a case to be made for scale for some clients and work types, this is not inevitably the only or best type of organisation to meet all client needs.

The many ways to grow a law firm

Neville Eisenberg
Berwin Leighton Paisner LLP

1. Introduction

Like other businesses, law firms can grow in many different ways. Often, growth will be achieved through a gradual process of expanding resources to meet growing client requirements or through a series of pragmatic and opportunistic acquisitions of additional professionals. However, there are also frequent opportunities to accelerate growth in more aggressive ways.

The growth decisions made by the management team of a law firm will depend on a variety of factors, such as:

- the market position of the firm;
- the ambitions of the partners;
- the nature of the firm's clients;
- competitive pressures and the actions taken by competitor firms;
- the nature of the practice areas covered by the firm; and
- changes in the firm's competitive markets.

Those decisions will also depend on the firm's business model. Is the firm a specialist or a full service provider? Single office, national or international? Regional or global? Consideration of which business model to pursue will often depend on the firm's historical evolution, the interests and ambitions of the partners and the financial performance of the model employed.

Changes to the existing model should be driven by the firm's strategy. This should also determine whether growth is desirable and, if so, to what degree. Growth should be an objective only if it helps to achieve the strategic aims of the firm.

It is sometimes assumed that growth is a good thing in all circumstances, given many of the obvious advantages that scale can provide. Scale can allow a firm to invest in people and systems, and to realise the benefits of technology. In the legal sector, scale is sometimes a prequalification for certain work, such as corporate mergers and acquisition work, or cross-border work requiring multiple capabilities in multiple jurisdictions.

On the other hand, many successful niche firms offer a limited range of services to a well-defined market. When a boutique strategy is well executed, a depth of experience is obtained that enables the firm to gain a pricing advantage and build a high-value brand, which then consequently attracts the top talent in the area. Equally, boutique practices are often seen as leaders in an area. This helps them to consolidate market understanding and a leadership position. On the practical side, boutique practices rarely have the bureaucracy or issues of conflict often seen in full-service firms. However, specialist firms can be susceptible to market shifts, which can have a major impact on the business.

While boutique practices can be very successful, most larger firms employ a multi-dimensional model. This means that they focus on distinct market segments defined by geography, sector, business type or service line, or a combination of these, and build their business around these.

Geographical focus has become increasingly important over the last decade. Market conditions and the trend towards globalisation have amplified the number of firms pursuing a strategy of geographical expansion and a global offering. International expansion was historically the preserve of the larger UK firms, which have pursued an international focus since the 1970s. However, US firms are increasingly pursuing expansionist models, focusing on emerging economies in Asia, South America and Europe. Some market commentators now believe that to survive and succeed in the future, larger firms will need to become either truly global, mirroring what has occurred in other professional service markets, or strong niche players.[1]

The focus by many firms on geographical expansion, as well as building a multi-dimensional offering, indicates that growth is generally fundamental to realising strategic aims. Many other strategic priorities require growth. Some examples of these include:

- expanding into new strategic areas that are generally defined along the lines of practice or sector capabilities;
- expanding into new markets or pursuing of new business opportunities;
- pursuing market leadership, generally defined along the lines of practice or sector capabilities;
- pursuing additional market share, which requires growth unless the market is shrinking;
- redefining market profile and perception;
- developing new competencies in order to meet client needs, whether this is through expanding existing capabilities or acquiring new capabilities;
- realising the advantages of economies of scale;
- attracting and retaining top talent and thereby attracting better-quality work; and
- investing in infrastructure such as technology in order to improve service delivery and efficiency.

By way of example, through pursuing certain strategic priorities Berwin Leighton Paisner LLP has undergone substantial growth in the last 10 years. After undergoing a merger in 2001, the firm focused for a period on what it called a 'three-pillar strategy', building additional capabilities in three key areas: real estate, corporate and finance. The firm subsequently added to its strategic goals by acquiring capabilities in litigation and tax. The three pillars became five. Pursuing these strategies resulted

---

1   See Kevin Wheeler, "Taking a bigger slice of the pie", *Law Business Review*, August 2011 pp 8-12.

in significant growth over the period, with revenue increasing from £86 million to £229 million.

However, achieving year-on-year growth is not easy. According to analysis completed by Legal Business, only one-third of the *Legal Business* 100 managed to increase both turnover and profits by more than the average over the five years from 2006 to 2011.[2] Looking at the five-year revenue growth statistics of *Legal Week's* UK Top 25, only eight firms achieved more than 50% growth in the five-year period. Many of these firms achieved such rapid growth through mergers (which can be one of the quickest ways to achieve substantial growth) and strategies of aggressive international expansion.

In the rest of this chapter we explore the different ways to achieve growth and some of their respective challenges and merits.

2. Options for growth

The main ways in which growth may be achieved include:

- expanding the firm's operations organically through existing resources;
- investing in individuals or teams through lateral hiring;
- undertaking a merger or acquisition, or building a franchise model;
- expanding geographically, either by establishing new offices or by partnering with or acquiring existing operations;
- developing value-added or innovative new service offerings; and
- competing through price differentiation.

2.1 Organic growth

Organic growth is achieved through a firm using its own internal resources to enhance its sales and increase the output of its legal services in existing or new markets. It does not include growth via acquisition or merger. Given the reliance of professional services on individual expertise, building internal capabilities usually takes many years. Changes in capability and market position therefore tend to be possible only over the long term. Firms following a more aggressive growth strategy need to consider other options for growth. Nevertheless, if growth is the aim, a focus on organic growth is important because it helps to ensure a dynamic environment and usually requires an expanding client base, a positive internal culture and an improving market position.

To achieve successful organic growth, a firm needs to:

- recruit the best available graduates;
- invest in and foster a training programme and career framework;
- develop the most talented associates to partners;
- improve business development efforts and results;
- ensure a clear focus and expertise on key clients and industry sectors; and
- offer a superior quality of service.

It must also ensure that business service functions are aligned and support the

---

2   LB 217, p 64.

legal service, as well as give an adequate picture of the state of the business through proper financial reporting and accountability.

Clarity over where support resources should be allocated is essential. As with any business, resources that cover too many priorities often cannot accomplish their objectives. One commonly expressed concern about full service firms is the potential for their resources to be stretched too thinly, resulting in the firm struggling to find a point of differentiation.[3] It is necessary, therefore, to have a clear focus and channel internal abilities towards a manageable number of areas and initiatives. As price pressures in the sector increase, some people argue that the justification for a price premium will be eroded if firms cannot differentiate their services.[4]

Some of the challenges with managing organic growth include:

- managing partners, who are both the owners and managers of the firm and income-producing professionals. A balance must be struck between a central management team providing leadership and direction and ensuring that sufficient communication and discussion occurs at a partnership level on key decisions;
- overcoming the experience glass ceiling. Clients value experience and are often understandably reluctant to give work to those who do not have it. It is difficult for a firm without expertise to gain it, as firms rarely get the chance from clients to build new expertise. It is not an impossible task – lawyers who are trusted advisers may well be trusted to handle new areas because of their overall relationship with a client. However, in general it can take a long time to expand into new areas and convince the market of the new capability through organic growth alone; and
- providing and upgrading the infrastructure and business service support at the right time in the growth cycle. Most law firms distribute all of their profits annually, which leaves little or no opportunity to build up a fund for future investment. This means that every investment decision is weighed against the immediate distribution of profits and any investment needs a clear rationale. During a period of active growth, there are generally clear points when it is essential to upgrade the infrastructure in order to take the firm to the next level of sophistication. Because partners tend to focus on short-term profit levels, they do not always appreciate the importance of a large new investment.

2.2 Growth through acquiring talent

Given that organic growth is usually a long-term strategy, firms that desire more rapid growth will usually hire partners and associates from other firms. In this way they can both acquire new capability and deepen and strengthen their existing capability. In fact, most firms will hire other lawyers from time to time – this is called 'lateral hiring'. This may take place on an occasional opportunistic basis or as part of a strategic growth programme.

In the decade after its merger in 2001, Berwin Leighton Paisner pursued an

---

3   Kevin Wheeler, "Taking a bigger slice of the pie", *Law Business Review* August 2011 pp 8-12.
4   Kevin Wheeler, "Taking a bigger slice of the pie", *Law Business Review* August 2011 pp 8-12.

extensive lateral hiring programme as part of its growth and transformation strategy. Focusing initially on real estate, corporate and finance, and later adding litigation and tax, the firm hired almost 100 new partners. The programme gave Berwin Leighton Paisner additional capabilities in areas where it was not previously strong, deepened existing strong practice areas and brought it new client relationships.

Hiring lateral recruits is also a common strategy for entering new markets, in terms of both geographical expansion and service area expansion. For example, many US firms have entered the London market over the last two decades through aggressive lateral hiring from established UK firms. US firms accounted for 540[5] of the 1,944 partner moves in London between 2005 and 2010.[6]

While lateral hiring can be a successful strategy, it is also complicated and has its challenges. Lateral recruits do not always remain with the hiring firm, which can make it a costly exercise with limited return. Research into lateral moves in the London market has shown that 33% of partners left the firm they joined after three years and 44% of the partners had left after five years.[7] Some of the key considerations in making the process a success include:

- ensuring that there is agreement about the role, experience and qualities required and about the expectations and measurable targets;
- ensuring that there is cultural alignment between the firm and the individual;
- having a clear and rigorous recruitment procedure, making sure to include management and all relevant partners;
- undertaking effective due diligence on candidates to validate their background, expertise, client list and portability of relationships; and
- ensuring successful integration into the firm, with time spent involving new hires on client matters, client development and supporting the sharing of ideas and input.

Another challenge is to ensure that the firm's external market reputation makes the firm attractive to desired candidates. In order to be attractive, the firm needs to have an existing platform in terms of client base, reputation and expertise, as well as the right culture.

2.3. Growth through merger and acquisition

A key strategic move for a law firm is to expand through a merger. This can generate significant benefits – complementary strategic areas or capabilities – depending on the nature of the parties to the merger. These in turn can expand:

- the client offering and service capabilities;

---

5   "Lateral Partner Moves in London", Motive Legal Consulting, http://www.motivelegal.com/index.php/downloads/.

6   Lateral hires are often combined with other growth programmes. Of the top lateral hires from non-UK firms over the last four years from 2006 to 2011 – which include Reed Smith with 32 lateral recruits, K&L Gates with 25 and Mayer Brown with 24 – all are US firms which have merged with UK firms in the last decade.

7   "Lateral Partner Moves in London", Motive Legal Consulting, http://www.motivelegal.com/index.php/downloads/.

- new capabilities or depth of experience within an existing area or sector, which can result in a shift in market profile and perception;
- the expansion of geographic coverage; and
- a realisation of economies of scale, depending on the size of the merging entities.

There have been some significant recent mergers in the legal sector. For example, UK firm Norton Rose merged with Deacons, one of Australia's largest law firms, in 2010 and then in 2011 with Canadian firm Ogilvy Renault and South African firm Deneys Reitz. The combined Norton Rose Group will be one of the world's 10 largest law firms, with a headcount of more than 2,500 lawyers. Another example is the transatlantic merger between UK firm Lovells and US firm Hogan & Hartson in 2010, which also created a top 10 global practice with 40 offices and around 2,500 lawyers.[8]

Berwin Leighton Paisner itself is the result of a number of mergers. The first was a merger between Berwin & Co, which joined the four-partner Leighton & Co in 1970 to form Berwin Leighton. Subsequently, Berwin Leighton merged with Paisner & Co in 2001. In 2009, Berwin Leighton Paisner 'merged' with a large team of 70 Moscow-based lawyers led by Andrey Goltsblat.

When a merger works well, it is the quickest way to gain capabilities and scale. The merger that created Berwin Leighton Paisner resulted in the legacy firms moving from individual revenues of £55.3 million for Berwin Leighton and £24 million for Paisner & Co and rankings in the *Legal Business* 100 in 2000 of 25 and 62 respectively, to a combined turnover of £87.4 million a year later and a ranking of 17.[9]

It took some time for the Berwin Leighton Paisner merger to consolidate and realise its benefits. The process was not helped by the economic downturn later the same year. As the following quotation in the 2001-2 edition of *Chambers* shows, the market's reaction to the merger was positive but low key: "Early days for this newly merged firm, but the initial signs are promising. Berwin Leighton, with its core strengths in property, sought to beef up its corporate practice by merging with Paisner, a field where the latter had a strong reputation."

The market shifted its perception of the firm's capabilities within a year. The 2002-3 *Chambers* edition reported: "Plans to move to a single site indicate that the year-old merger with Paisner has settled down well. The union has achieved the aim of broadening out the firm's client base. In corporate finance matters the diversity is apparent. ... Real estate and its related specialisms continue to be areas in which the firm excels. ... Links to the property market have also ensured a profile for its hotel and leisure team. ... The firm has grown since the merger, and clients were keen to stress that it has retained its partner-led approach."

Given the complexity of merging two law firms, many such discussions do not crystallise into a merger. This might help to explain the low rate of sector consolidation compared to other professional services. The largest players in the

---

8   "Hogan Lovells", *Legal Week*, December 14 2009 and Jeremy Hodges, "Lovells and Hogan & Hartson size up high-stakes transatlantic merger", *Legal Week*, October 2009.

9   LB 108, September 2000, The 2000 *Legal Business* 100 & LB 117, September 2001, The *2001 Legal Business 100*.

sector still hold only 1% to 2% of the entire market.[10]

Putting aside these complexities, there are several other key considerations:

- Financial integration – often, difficulties lie in the fact that there are material differences in the profitability between practice areas and locations, or differences in methods of calculating profit and modes of distribution. It is not an attractive prospect for the partners who need to vote on the merger to face either smaller earnings in the short term or a difficult and protracted process of integrating two systems of remuneration. For this reason, some recent mergers are not fully integrated financially, but instead use separate entities with no single profit pool.[11] A Swiss *Verein* structure is often used, which allows firms to maintain separate financial profit pools while integrating other aspects of their business and operating under a single brand. Some argue that the Swiss *Verein* removes one of the major barriers to merger activity – widely different profit levels – and that the flexibility it offers increases the strategic merger choices now available to firms.[12] Others argue that a merger is incomplete until the firms are fully integrated, including financially. Even if there is no financial integration, the merged entities still have the challenge of creating a global brand and consistent client service across the global footprint.

- Issues of client conflict – these include conflicts arising from professional ethics rules and commercial conflicts. Resolving these conflicts can take up a significant proportion of senior personnel time.

- Cultural differences – this is generally a threshold consideration for any merger discussion. Losing a distinct culture and having an alien one imposed is often a great concern. If the cultures are not naturally aligned or the integration is not well managed, there is a risk of lawyer attrition after completion. This can considerably undermine the prospects of success.

- Integration costs and difficulties – integrating two separate firms requires agreement on some fundamental issues. These include the merging of management, IT systems, business services infrastructure and premises. Staff and partner rationalisation and rebranding can also be complex. Integration generally also needs to cover remuneration and profit. However, as discussed above, this depend on the legal structure used to establish the merged entity and is not always necessary.

- Convincing the partnership – sufficient partner consensus must be established before proceeding with any merger. Gaining the required support can be a significant hurdle. The partnership structure and requirement for a vote effectively means that if sufficient partners are not supportive it becomes very difficult to close the transaction.

When Berwin Leighton and Paisner & Co merged in 2001 the integration

---

10   See revenue figures of the Global 100 from LB 217, September 2011.
11   "When is a merger not a merger?", *The Chambers Magazine*, Autumn 2010, pp 4.
12   Andrew Hedley, "New Directions", *LIM legal* 2011, 5(4), pp 26-27.

strategy was planned well in advance. It was considered important to gain buy-in across the firm and there was active communication with all staff afterwards to establish a feeling of belonging. The integration team worked hard to ensure that every individual from the two businesses felt valued and part of the new entity. The team was aware of the dangers of having anyone feel isolated. The HR team in particular ensured that all groups were consulted on the detailed integration plan.

A business planning process was put in place for all departments, with a focus on key goals for the coming year. Forward-looking objectives for departments and groups helped to speed up the process of integration. The departmental-level planning exercise was followed by a broader, firm-wide project around the firm's strategic direction. This ensured that all staff were involved in forming the vision and strategic goals for Berwin Leighton Paisner.

The new firm's management team considered it critical that the integration exercise be completed quickly. A team of directors was established to work on it. They completed most of the detailed integration planning before the merger went live. All systems, including IT and financial systems, were ready to go live on the effective date. On the day of the merger, all lawyers arrived at the office to a common email address and new business cards.

It was important to avoid the symbolic continuation of two separate businesses, so the offices were rapidly physically integrated. Individuals from the two firms were physically relocated to ensure physical integration within departments. To aid social integration, many social events were organised before and after the merger.

2.4 The franchise model

Another way for firms to expand their reach is for them to use a franchise model. In this arrangement the franchisee pays to be part of a franchise. This gives it the right to use the brand name, provided that it conforms with clearly defined business management procedures and standards. Easily recognisable franchises are McDonald's and Subway. In the legal sector the concept has had a more fluid application and there is debate as to the degree to which certain law firms are really franchise operations. The franchise model may also be useful for some of the new law firm structures that have become possible under the Legal Services Act.[13]

An interesting example of how the franchise model can evolve is Eversheds. This firm grew from a loose group of different practices with their own geographical and departmental management structures.[14] This meant that each firm operated as a single profit centre and all of the firms contributed an amount each year to a central fund.[15] However, over time moves were made to create a more unified existence. In 1995 the offices adopted a single name; set up billing and profit criteria for each region, which led to closer financial convergence; and established uniform standards in client handling, management training and information technology.[16] During the

---

13   Alisa Dixon, "McLaw v the Supersizers – is the future for law firms really as a franchise?", SJ 154/39, 19 October 2010.

14   "Eversheds: firm or franchise?", *Legal Business*, issue 55, June 1995, pp 54.

15   "Eversheds: firm or franchise?", *Legal Business*, issue 55, June 1995, pp 55.

16   "Eversheds moves from franchise to firm", *Legal Business*, issue 105, pp 26.

1980s and 1990s the firms merged. Finally, in 2000 the financial and management structures were fully integrated across all of the 13 UK offices.[17]

This strategy – combining strong regional firms under a common banner into one national entity – resulted in considerable growth for Eversheds. In the *Legal Business* 100 rankings, the firm moved from a ranking of 39 to a ranking of five within four years, and from a turnover of £22.1 million in 1995 to a turnover of £212.4 million in 2000. It also saw a corresponding increase in partners, from 34 in 1995 to 201 in 2000.[18]

A more recent example of the franchise-type model is Quality Solicitors. This firm operates at the consumer end of the market. Quality Solicitors began with a lead referral method with the aim of weaving together disparate, independent high-street law firms under a national brand. Members paid a fee for a pooled marketing budget and enquiries from the Quality Solicitors website were divided up among members.[19] More recently, Quality Solicitors has changed its model to a more typical franchise set-up, in which members pay an annual membership fee.

The franchise model has enabled Quality Solicitors to build within two years a business with a turnover of £8 million and a membership of 170 firms. It also has a tie-in with WHSmith that could see the company set up 500 high-street stores.[20] It is still to be seen whether this or other emerging business models in the consumer sector, such as Face2Face Solicitors and HighStreetLawyer.com, will ultimately be successful. The challenges of the franchise model will need to be overcome in order to successfully build a consumer legal brand that equates to consistent service delivery and quality.

2.5 Growth through geographical expansion

Law firms have for many years sought ways to expand into new geographical regions. Today, many of the largest UK firms, for example, generate more than 50% of their revenue from overseas.[21]

Key drivers for geographical expansion generally fall into one of the following categories:

- the pursuit of new market opportunities. As an example, in 2010, 44 of the top 50 US law firms had a presence in China. Yet 17 of those firms had only opened their offices since 2005.[22] This growth was motivated by a sense that there were many new opportunities in the Hong Kong and other Asian equity capital markets;
- limited growth prospects in the domestic market, whether due to a saturated or stagnating market;
- satisfying client requirements. As clients expand their businesses into new locations, so do their legal needs expand; or

---

17   Eversheds website, http://www.eversheds.com/
18   *Legal Business* Magazine, October series from 1995-2000.
19   "Street Smart", *Legal Business*, issue 215, p 37.
20   "Street Smart", *Legal Business*, issue 215, p 38.
21   LB July/August 2011 – LB216, pp 70.
22   "CHINA: US firms on the rise", *The Chambers Magazine*, Summer 2010, pp 18–21.

- competitive pressures. As more firms seek to provide a global service, other firms are pressured to copy them in order to remain competitive.

There are a number of ways in which to expand internationally, including:
- with the firm's own offices;
- through an alliance or best-friend relationship; or
- through a merger with a local office.

Firms will employ some or all of these options depending on the particularities of the local market and their own market position, capabilities, client base and investment options. All of them have their relative merits and challenges.

Berwin Leighton Paisner has pursued all of these options at various times, in part due to having two parallel international strategies.

(a) *Geographical expansion – opening new offices*

One strand of Berwin Leighton Paisner's international growth strategy focuses on emerging markets. Over the last five years the firm has opened several new offices – in Singapore in 2007, Abu Dhabi and Moscow in 2009, and more recently in Hong Kong and Germany.

Opening an office in another jurisdiction has many challenges and the road to success can be rocky. It is wise to keep in mind:
- a clear understanding of why the firm is expanding into the particular market. This should be aligned with the firm's strategy, the desired service offering and capabilities – including how these differ from the existing local services – and measures of success;
- a thorough understanding of the local market, the demand and supply for legal services and an understanding of the local culture and ways of doing business. It is very important not to be inadvertently offensive or insensitive towards your future colleagues;
- the support and buy-in of the partnership, including any required investment, which may be substantial and long term. The early involvement of partners ensures support for the initiative and a rigorous analysis of the opportunity and financial forecasts from the start;
- a team with the correct mix of local capabilities and 'home-based' capabilities. This ensures local knowledge and credibility, as well as integration with the rest of the firm and operational consistency between offices. Project management is essential for coordinating the practicalities of opening an office and business development capabilities are essential for growing the business; and
- flexibility to refine the strategy according to market conditions and the progress achieved.

(b) *Geographical expansion – establishing a preferred firm/alliance network*

The second strand has been the establishment of a group of preferred firms through which to provide services to its clients. Berwin Leighton Paisner has built close relationships with a panel of leading independent firms from 65 different countries. Thanks to this arrangement the firm can provide its clients with a seamless and efficient service across multiple jurisdictions. The relationships are non-exclusive, which means that Berwin Leighton Paisner can use different offices according to the needs of the client or job. Building the structures, tools and processes needed to manage, communicate and develop these relationships has been a significant task.

There are many reasons why firms choose to establish an alliance or a network rather than pursue the other modes of expansion. In the case of Berwin Leighton Paisner, it was considered the best way to provide clients with a high-quality service across multiple jurisdictions. Other firms may find that the size of the market does not warrant a standalone office; client demand is better served by the local market, a boutique or domestic market strategy and needs only an alliance to be able to refer clients to; or simply local regulations make it difficult or impossible to establish a local presence.

Establishing an alliance network, preferred firm group or series of best-friend relationships also has its challenges. Issues to consider include:

- ensuring that a network, best-friend relationship or alliance fits the firm's strategy and is not a standalone activity;
- understanding whether the intention of building relationships is to seek referrals or to develop a more client-focused partnership;
- being clear about whether support services, knowledge and training will be shared, or teams combined, to provide the service. The relationship must benefit both parties;
- appreciating the capabilities and quality of work of the partner firm. Any work from an alliance partner must meet the quality associated with your brand and expected by your client;
- appreciating how long it takes to build the relationship. Any relationship based on personal chemistry and trust takes time and effort to develop. A programme should be put in place to develop personal relationships at all levels of the firm, from associates to partners and across business services;
- considering how to create a seamless service, or perception of seamlessness, across a network. This includes uniform terms of engagement, insurance cover, single points of contact and building relationships across firms and between firms in the network;
- investing in tools and systems to help build the network, service it and promote it internally;
- managing risk and liability. This includes being clear about the terms of engagement, ensuring that a clear process exists for transferring instructions and, at the start, completing sufficient due diligence, providing insurance protection and building strong relationships; and
- ensuring that whatever arrangement is put in place, you remain flexible enough to meet your individual client's needs.

2.6 Growth through new services or adding value
Another option for growth arises when a firm differentiates itself through additional

service offerings or value-added extras and so expands its market share. Many professional services offer free audits or reviews, and law firms are considering other innovative ways to add value. In 2006 Addleshaw Goddard, for example, launched its Client Development Centre. This pulled together a range of value-added services, including an IT tool set.[23] Eversheds has launched a consulting service for in-house counsel as a means of deepening relationships with its current clients and offering a broader range of services. On a smaller scale, one firm based in Bath has recently launched a private client service in Hong Kong, focused on the expatriate market. In addition to the typical private client services, it offers to pay clients' bills, sort out their tax returns and even move their elderly parents into care homes in the United Kingdom.[24]

Berwin Leighton Paisner creates additional value for clients through a number of offerings. One example is Lawyers on Demand (LOD), which launched in 2007 on a contract basis. LOD sought to address two trends: clients wanted to stretch their budgets for legal services, while at the same time many lawyers were looking for greater flexibility and autonomy in their work. LOD brings freelance lawyers to work directly with clients. All of the lawyers are vetted by Berwin Leighton Paisner, which supports them in any assignment with knowledge and resources. When it began as a pilot, LOD started with eight lawyers. It now has a team of approximately 80, The business has grown rapidly and within four years has a turnover of more than £5 million.

A second example at Berwin Leighton Paisner is the Managed Legal Service. In 2010 Berwin Leighton Paisner agreed to provide Thames Water with the majority of the legal services required for a five-year term in return for a fixed revenue. As part of the deal, the majority of the Thames Water legal team transferred to Berwin Leighton Paisner.

The idea behind the Managed Legal Service is for Berwin Leighton Paisner to take over all, or a discrete part, of a client's legal needs and deliver those services for a known fee. The three main objectives are cost savings, budget certainty and guaranteed performance standards. The key is for Berwin Leighton Paisner to source the legal work efficiently, alongside a bespoke operating platform. The aim is to encourage efficiencies in both the management and provision of legal work.

With any value-added service, it is essential to:

- understand the client need that the service seeks to address and make sure that it does this;
- market the service effectively so that the target clients know and understand it; and
- listen to client feedback and adapt or modify the offering as appropriate.

---

23   Addleshaw Goddard website, http://www.addleshawgoddard.com/cdc/view.asp?content_id=2461 &parent_id=2422.

24   "Business Strategies Client Services: Riding the tiger, managing partner Derwent Campbell reveals how Mogers launched its new private client service in Hong Kong", *Managing Partner*, July/August 2011, pp 24.

2.7   Growth through price differentiation

One of the other key ways to grow is through price differentiation. Low-cost airline carriers, for example, offer cheaper fares by maximising their operations. In this way they reduce costs and therefore have a significantly lower operating cost structure than their competitors. It is arguable that a true price differentiation strategy has not yet been seen in the legal sector. However, the sector is feeling increasing pressure on fees and many firms now offer alternate billing arrangements.

A *Legal Week* report on the outsourcing of legal processes, released in May 2011, indicated that the most common way for law firms to reduce costs is to offer alternative fee structures. This occurs in 75.1% of the firms surveyed. This was followed by staffing initiatives, IT innovation, outsourcing of legal processes and finally outsourcing of business processes.[25]

As firms increasingly compete on price, several alternative billing structures have become common. These include blended rates, price capping, price collaring, contingent fees and success fees. Law firms are also trying to reduce their operating costs through outsourcing back office functions. In some cases they are also outsourcing their less complex legal work. Some firms have concentrated on large-volume work and have used investment and economies of scale to build capabilities on a large scale and expand their service offering through acquisitions. Some corporate law firms have hired external price consultants to increase the sophistication of their pricing and ability to offer different and varied pricing options.

Legal service outsourcers have also changed the competitive dynamic in the sector. Clients can now outsource the more routine and less complex elements of legal work, especially the document reviews required in due diligence and discovery processes.

3.   The Legal Services Act 2007

Much has been written about the impact of deregulation in the legal sector and the impact of the Legal Services Act. While certain firms, mainly in the consumer arena, have expressed an interest in the changes allowed under the act, such as forming an alternate business structure, pursuing external funding and appointing non-legal managers and owners, it is still uncertain how deregulation will affect the corporate law sector. So far, the corporate market has shown only limited interest in making changes in ownership and management or taking on external funding. However, the additional flexibility for investment could provide firms with the funds to aid expansion. The coming years may therefore see firms undergoing rapid growth as numerous options are pursued. On the other hand, given the resistance to change in the corporate law sector, more conservative commentators predict that the effect will be more subtle, with firms initially adopting an increasingly 'corporate' approach to governance, internal management and reporting.

4.   Conclusion

While growth can be a fundamental part of realising strategic aims, it is no substitute

---

25   Legal Week – Benchmarker, *Legal Week Intelligence*, May 2011.

for a good strategy. Growth is merely one of a set of tools and potential outcomes that can result from the strategy adopted.

The author would like to thank Yolanda Zollinger, business manager at Berwin Leighton Paisner, for her assistance in writing this chapter.

Effective PR strategies for the succcessful law firm

Sean Twomey
Norton Rose LLP

1. Introduction

Good PR wins work, adds value to client relationships and puts the spotlight on lawyers' expertise. Over the last decade, legal PR has improved its own profile and gained credibility among lawyers in terms of its power to protect and enhance reputation. However, the primary driver has not been the ability of PR to aid business development or showcase a firm's expertise. In general, rather than seeing its potential, fear and lack of confidence in dealing with the media have forced firms to become more professional in how they handle media relations. Taking a more positive approach and developing a culture that understands how to work with the press can reap significant benefits for any law firm, large or small.

1.1. The evolution of PR in the legal profession

In general, most highly regarded law firms will have a managed media profile. Some firms and partners have clearly embraced the potential of PR, while others have done very little. My own view is that the legal profession is generally still in the early stages of its PR evolution. Law firms are unlikely to be as advanced in this respect as publicly listed corporations, which have legal and regulatory disclosure requirements, a management with roles and responsibilities for media relations and an experienced PR function.

1.2 Lawyers and journalists: a mutually beneficial match

Nevertheless, the legal profession is well suited to PR (subject to client confidentiality, of course). This is because the media is always interested in risk, doubt, conflict and/or uncertainty, and lawyers are expected to advise in these circumstances. Journalists, especially those writing about business, find lawyers' opinions useful in guiding them to what they should be reporting on. This mutually beneficial relationship underlines why the legal profession should be so much better at utilising the potential of PR.

1.3 How to move PR up a gear in your firm

Slowly but surely, the legal profession is recognising the benefits and potential of good media relations. In my work as a PR professional for the last 15 years, I have always tried to develop a culture of working with the press. I encourage lawyers to use it as a marketing tool. This has included developing best practices for working with journalists and PR protocols for crisis management situations, training lawyers to highlight their expertise in the media and establishing PR campaigns to support business development.

The following sections are designed to help to achieve these goals and should prove useful to management, the PR function (if one already exists) and/or any partner or lawyer who wants to use PR, regardless of whether the firm is highly evolved in this respect or just starting on this road.

2. The role of PR in a law firm

Every one of the 100 international law firms listed by *Legal Business* features a PR/media contact on its website. The resources that each dedicates to PR and how effectively it manages its media relations will vary, but there is no doubt that interaction with the media is something that law firms seek to manage. The approach to PR will be different and its importance will vary according to the attitude of management, the aptitude of the partners, the PR team and the significance of good media relations in the market(s) in which the firm operates. Nevertheless, the following should be common to every law firm:

- the drivers for law firms to manage their PR;
- the role of management;
- the role of partners; and
- the PR function.

2.1 The drivers for law firms to manage their PR

(a) Integrity

Integrity and perceived professionalism are of paramount value to a law firm. It is therefore unsurprising that many firms seek to protect their reputation and enhance it in the media. Every law firm will be judged in part by what clients, staff, potential employees, competitors and the media read about it. The library of information on the Internet, and particularly the use of Google, also mean that what is written is easily searchable and lasts longer than the hard copy in which it was published. This is particularly important for potential new recruits doing their research for an interview or due diligence when an offer has been made.

(b) Cost effectiveness

Good media relations and good PR can be very cost effective when compared with advertising. It is also regarded as more objective and independent than advertising. In the words of Richard Branson, "Using yourself to get out and talk about it is a lot cheaper and more effective than a lot of advertising. In fact, if you do it correctly, it can beat advertising hands down and save tens of millions of dollars."

(c) Prudence

Building media relationships can also be a prudent part of a defensive strategy. For large law firms, unwanted and negative stories are inevitable. Whether they are serious and undermine the integrity of the brand or are irritating but relatively harmless, a law firm will from time to time have to deal with stories that it wishes had not been published. If relationships already exist with the publications or the journalists writing these stories, this will help to limit the potential damage that they can cause. It can also sometimes provide an opportunity to neutralise what is written. Equally, if those tasked with dealing with the media are trained and prior consideration has been given to using a PR agency, then a law firm is much better prepared to deal with a crisis.

2.2 The role of management

(a) Responsibility

As in any organisation, everyone at a law firm is responsible for ensuring that its reputation is not damaged or detrimentally affected by their actions. Responsibility within a law firm for enhancing the brand and positively building the brand lies predominately with the business development function, the partnership and, in particular, the management.

(b) Training

It is advisable that those in management be trained to deal with the media. This is especially important for new management partners. Too often they are expected just to know what to do when a journalist calls. Media training needs to cover everything from the most basic etiquette when speaking to a journalist to dealing with a crisis management situation. (Media training is covered in more detail below.)

(c) Management issues

Management issues must be dealt with by senior management only. These might be anything that has implications across the firm. Issues such as employment disputes (which can attract significant media interest), law firm strategy, financial performance and remuneration should all be the responsibility of senior management and not the personal opinions of partners. It is the responsibility of the PR function to clarify who should deal with what before the need arises.

(d) PR philosophy

In any law firm, the philosophy for dealing with the media will be influenced by management. Senior management can influence and encourage effective PR by recognising and encouraging partners and staff when they achieve positive coverage for themselves and the firm. This should be done consistently and should seek to reinforce a culture of positive PR. At the same time, individuals should never be criticised because they achieve excellent coverage for themselves and the firm. This is called 'tall poppy syndrome'. In some cultures it describes when people are criticised for their success because it elevates them above or distinguishes them from their peers. Even as a joke, this negative sentiment should be discouraged.

2.3 The role of partners – who should do the PR within a law firm

(a) Responsibility

Partners have a responsibility to make sure that the rules and best practices for how to deal with the press, as laid out by management, are followed. While management issues are the responsibility of senior partners, the spokespeople for highlighting a law firm's expertise should predominately be its partners. Partners with legal expertise should use the media to promote their practice. The best lawyers will not just interpret the law, but seek to influence it. For these lawyers in particular, the media has tremendous potential – not just as a way of promoting their expertise, but also as an advocate for their clients.

From my experience, lawyers fall into one of three categories in their dealings with the media: they are doves, hawks or chickens. These three attitudes reflect the full spectrum of partners' approaches when asked to react to an inquiry from the media or encouraged to be proactive in highlighting their expertise.

Doves: The doves recognise the importance of working with the media. They are savvy in dealing with journalists and instinctively understand the etiquette involved. They need little guidance and understand when they can comment and how to say nothing if they should not comment. The doves are PR naturals and are internally recognised for their ability to communicate effectively. The motivation for them to do PR will vary, but they recognise that it can help them to build their practice. In an average partnership, only around 20% of partners might be classified as doves.

Hawks: The hawks do not recognise the importance of working with the media. The most extreme are dismissive and arrogant when asked to do so. They don't return calls, they question the value of engagement and they want to dictate what is reported rather than seek to influence by building up relationships. As law firm PR has evolved, the hawks have become fewer and their influence is diminishing. Yet they still make up at least 10% of an average partnership. Unless hawks are in senior management, in which case they need training, I would not prioritise hawks for PR work.

Chickens: On average 70% – the vast majority – of partners are chickens. This term is not intended to be discourteous. It reflects a fear and hesitation in dealing with the media, but not a reluctance to get it right. Most chickens want to be doves, but it just doesn't come naturally. They want to be trained and encouraged to use media relations to develop their practice. This is where time, resources and training should be spent educating partners in PR. The PR function and or business development function should concentrate accordingly on developing the 'chicken' partners.

2.4   The PR function

(a)   What is the PR function?
The PR function is a firm's PR team, if one exists. If it doesn't, it is the business development or the marketing person or people responsible for it. The PR function will vary enormously from firm to firm, but if it exists it will support the partnership. In particular, it should work with those partners who want to use the media and need help to do so.

(b)   ***The role of the PR function***

The role of the PR function is to guide senior management and partners to improve and protect the firm's reputation. It is assumed that when someone is given the responsibility of managing PR, they are tasked with dealing with the press. This is key, of course, but in fact the most challenging and rewarding aspect of the role is teaching the partnership to deal effectively with the media themselves. Turning chickens into doves isn't easy, but it is what makes a good PR most valuable.

The PR function needs to suit its approach to each partner. All partners can do PR, but how they do it should be tailored to their abilities, their aptitude, the sector and market in which they work and their own preferences. Some partners would love to learn how to do television interviews, for example, while others enjoy writing articles.

(c)   ***How the PR function can facilitate relationships between partners and journalists***

The PR function must understand both the business of a law firm and the nature of a publication and journalist in order to facilitate relationships between partners and the media. Journalists are generally under pressure to file stories. This is exacerbated for some by the immediacy of news expected by the Internet. If the PR function can match partners' experience, expertise and knowledge with what journalists have to report on, then it will successfully facilitate relationships. Giving a news journalist information for stories enables him or her to write something. The more information given, the more highly valued the PR function becomes as a contact, and the more leverage it will have as to what is written about the firm. As the poet and civil servant Humbert Wolfe once put it:

> *You cannot hope to bribe or twist,*
> *thank God! the British journalist.*
> *But, seeing what the man will do*
> *unbribed, there's no occasion to.*

There is a predictability to what journalists will want and when. How they work differs depending on the type of medium – if it is a daily, weekly or monthly publication, and whether it is news or a feature that is being written. However, there is sufficient consistency for a good PR function to know whether it can help. It is this ability to add value for the journalist in doing their job that determines the strength of the relationship.

3.   The five levels of PR

The following section seeks to outline the criteria for assessing a firm's PR sophistication. Level 1 is the most essential and basic PR; level 5 is the most advanced and sophisticated.

The levels are a generalisation. At any one time the PR function may be undertaking an activity at level 5, but if the basics at level 1 are not being undertaken, then future PR will be random and *ad hoc* rather than planned and strategic.

Categories have been defined within each level, separating activities into four groups, including administrative best practice, news management and crisis management.

3.1 Level 1: the foundations

The foundations are the source for information and understanding as to what should be promoted. If undertaken thoroughly and comprehensively, there are also other significant benefits from an internal communications and business development perspective.

Experience, expertise and deal information should be collected and searchable for the following outlets:

- league tables (eg, M&A league tables);
- directories;
- deals databases;
- websites;
- internal profiles;
- experience statements;
- marketing materials; and
- annual reports.

At this level, the PR function should know what is being written about the firm and who is doing what in terms PR activity. They should be recognised internally as responsible for coordinating PR and be a point of contact, especially for the legal and trade press.

(a) Level 1 checklist: PR function roles and responsibilities

Administrative best practice:

- Has an established process for collecting experience, expertise and information on deals;
- Knows how and when to promote internally and externally;
- Has a system for collecting and distributing media coverage to relevant partners; and
- Understands the importance of photography, with up-to-date photos of partners in house style.

News and profile management:

- Knows what is going on;
- Is an internal point of contact for PR; and
- Assists partners who are interested in raising their profile.

Crisis management:

- Is able to recognise a potential negative story.

3.2 Level 2: reactive

At this level the PR function is able to react competently to internal and external media requests.

PR activity at level 2 possesses the information to respond efficiently to the following:

- servicing partners who want to do PR;
- coordinating directory entries;
- drafting press releases;
- responding to media enquiries; and
- recognising bad news stories and potential bad news.

(a)   *Level 2 checklist: PR function roles and responsibilities*

Administrative best practice:
- Keeps accurate records of PR activity (eg cuttings files, meetings held and upcoming, press releases and so on);
- Can draft press releases and knows how to identify journalists and publications who will write about the firm;
- Keeps an accurate and up-to-date list of relevant journalists; and
- Can manage the directory process.

News and profile management:
- Helps partners to raise their profile by contacting identified journalists and publications;
- Understands how to handle media inquiries made of the firm;
- Prepares directory submissions and organises partner interviews; and
- Prepares submissions for awards with guidance from partners.

Crisis management:
- Is able to recognise a potential negative news story and raise it with management accordingly.

3.3   Level 3: managing PR

PR starts to become exciting at level 3. At this level, the firm's PR function and partners are beginning to view PR opportunities as positive for developing the business.

What distinguishes level 3 from 2 is that the PR is being managed rather than being task led. The PR function is able to lead rather than being told what to do by the partnership.

The following are examples:
- PR provides advice to partners and facilitaties good relationships and manages poor relationships with the media;
- PR understands what constitutes a positive opportunity;
- Relationships are being built with the media;
- The 'dove' partners are being helped to excel at PR;
- The PR function knows how to pitch ideas that may generate stories and features;
- Journalists are using the firm as a first point of call; and
- PR can measure improvements in coverage, in particular the volume of positive coverage in key publications.

(a) Level 3 checklist: PR function roles and responsibilities

Administrative best practice:
- There is a system for monitoring, categorising and measuring the firm's media coverage;
- PR plans are being drafted and used to guide partners as to how to raise their profile;
- Partners are being trained in how to work with the press;
- Senior management have been given responsibility for various firm-wide issues; and
- The PR function meets partners to encourage meetings with journalists, press releases and ideas to pitch.

News and profile management:
- Can draft and follow up press releases with phone calls to journalists;
- Is starting to build relationships with the legal, trade and national press and broadcast media in which the firm is recognised for its expertise;
- Can distinguish between what is newsworthy and what is not newsworthy;
- Can identify media issues on which partners will be able to comment on and connects partners with journalists;
- Has a proactive approach to directories, working with partners to identify underperforming areas and developing strategies to improve these rankings;
- Is actively looking for awards to enter; and
- Devises ideas for the media.

Crisis management:
- Is up to date with any internal developments that may result in negative coverage; and
- Recognises how to minimise negative media coverage by dealing with journalists.

3.4 Level 4: proactive, planned and strategic

At this level PR is being strategically managed. The key is that progress be agreed, planned and achieved. PR is therefore set measurable targets and progress is evaluated on a regular basis.

The key features of this level include:
- working with at least 80% of partners to improve their profile;
- devising, communicating and ensuring compliance with best practice protocols;
- adding value to business development;
- adopting a firm-wide approach to managing PR;
- planning for the annual calendar of directories, awards and forward features; and
- having a high degree of awareness of potential negative stories and vulnerabilities.

(a)   *Level 4 checklist: PR function roles and responsibilities*

Administrative best practice:
- A proactive approach to media relations is culturally encouraged by the PR function and adopted by the law firm;
- Those who achieve notable positive coverage are recognised; and
- A direct link can be made between PR and the strengthening of relationships with clients and potential new business opportunities.

News and profile management:
- Occasionally achieves high profile coverage, especially in the national press and broadcast media;
- Works with at least 80% of partners on profile-raising activities; Constantly identifies issues that may also be relevant across practice areas and departments;
- Achieves improved rankings in the agreed priority directories and measurable improvement in the volume of positive coverage;
- Trains partners who otherwise would not do PR to improve their expertise (turning chickens into doves); and
- Develops PR plans for practice areas and/or departments.

Crisis management:
- Has a thorough understanding of the firm and issues that are of interest for the media;
- Anticipates upcoming issues and alerts senior management to potential negative news stories; and
- Works to mitigate damage.

3.5   Level 5: campaign driven
The difference between levels 4 and 5 is that the PR is much more aligned to business development and the possibility of winning work through campaigns. On top of its day-to-day duties, the PR function also considers initiatives that will build a platform for winning new work from the firm's experience, expertise and know-how.

Campaigns provide a higher likelihood of opportunities for building a brand and profile in a particular area of expertise. PR at level 5 should feature the following:
- high-level buy-in from senior partners;
- excellent coordination with business development;
- PR at the highest end of media – namely, broadcast and national media;
- feedback from clients from PR and occasionally the provision of opportunities to win work;
- delivery of planned objectives; and
- demonstration that the PR function is achieving better coverage than its competitors.

(a) Level 5 checklist: PR function roles and responsibilities

Administrative best practice:
- There is a regular review of PR activity with the firm's management;
- Firm-wide understanding of and compliance with PR best practices. These would include:
  - drafting and communicating press releases;
  - devising and launching campaigns; and
  - managing the directory process;
- The PR function can compare objectively the profile and reputation of the firm against its competitors;
- PR resources and time are aligned with the best opportunities for business development; and
- The PR function works across the firm with business development and other support departments, including knowledge management, HR and finance.

News and profile management:
- Consistently achieves high-profile coverage in the legal, trade and national press and broadcast media;
- Exceeds the coverage given to major competitors in national and broadcast media;
- Can measure media activity and monitor progress and report on this to partners;
- Provides trusted PR and communications advice and training to the partnership;
- Devises, develops and leads campaigns; and
- Drafts, implements and reviews detailed PR plans for practice groups, practice areas and/or partners.

Crisis management:
- Firm-wide crisis management protocols are tested on a regular basis; and
- Protocols exist for categorising and subsequently managing negative stories.

4. Nurturing relationships with the media

There are too many misconceptions about what media training for lawyers involves. The common view is that it involves being taught how to deflect difficult questions from an aggressive journalist. This kind of training has its place and should be given to those senior managers who are likely to have to appear in public in times of crisis. But the majority of partners in a law firm just need a basic understanding of what is involved in raising their profile.

Establishing and maintaining contacts with journalists is one of the simplest, cheapest and most effective techniques. It also doesn't require any training.

4.1 Identifying target publications

The first step is to identify those publications in which you want to feature. They should include publications and media that your clients and prospective clients read, listen to or watch. For those in management, they should also include the legal press, which is enormously important to the profile of a law firm.

4.2 Follow the news

Once you are clear as to target publications and media, it is vital that you read, listen to or watch them. While this may be stating the obvious, it is surprising how often lawyers are not on the correct internal distributions or receive publications but don't read them.

The next step is to familiarise yourself with what makes news and what makes features for that publication. Every publication will have criteria for what it considers more prominent news. Understanding what makes a publication's front page and what is given only a small mention is key. The division of the publication into different sections is also important; as is identifying which journalists write about what. Relationships cannot be properly established unless a publication is analysed in this way.

4.3 Identify a key journalist

Once you have identified a target journalist, consider how you can add value to what he or she has previously written or reported on. A good idea for lawyers is to scribble Post-it notes on articles that are interesting. This helps to provide material as to why a meeting or telephone call should be fixed with the journalist who has written the story or feature.

4.4 Build a relationship with the journalist

These are some tips for building a relationship with a journalist:

- Always work with your PR function. They will help you to fix calls, find contact details and assist with follow-up actions, such as meeting article deadlines.
- Schedule regular contact. Every three months, make contact with an email, brochure, telephone call, an umbrella, a lunch and so on. It is essential to keep yourself at the front of the journalist's mind. PR can help with this if necessary.
- Ask journalists for their views and don't hesitate to challenge them if you don't agree. Always ask questions – they can be a good source of information.
- Be clear as to what you can and can't talk about. Never talk about anything you wouldn't be happy to see in print. A common mistake is to talk off the record and not understand that it is perfectly acceptable for a journalist to report what you have mentioned 'off the record' as long as it is not attributed. Equally, don't be embarrassed to say that you don't know the answer to a question. But do say you will get back to them (and make sure you do), or refer them to other sources that may be helpful.
- Building a good working relationship with a journalist is not unlike dealing with a client. It needs to be mutually beneficial and built on trust, and perceived as honest and cooperative.

4.5   The PR function and media familiarisation

As with lawyers, the PR function must familiarise itself with all relevant media. The list of media concerning law firms can be vast. It reflects the range of sectors, industries and jurisdictions that are relevant to a client, together with all legal press that is important for the firm. It is unlikely that the PR function can regularly read, listen and watch everything that might be relevant, but it must at least be familiar with it. The most common complaint of journalists about PRs is that they don't understand their publication and what they will be interested in reporting on.

5.   Conclusion

The current changes in the legal profession will see the role and function of PR change significantly over the next decade. In its early days, the legal PR function acted as a gatekeeper, protecting management from enquiries and doing little more than issuing press releases.

Today, most law firms use PR to help build and promote their brand. Different firms operate at different levels and are at different stages in their PR evolution. Whether it is winning awards, improving legal directory rankings, achieving higher-profile positive coverage or devising PR campaigns with a view to winning work, law firms all want to be perceived as better than their competitors.

In the next decade, certain factors will further accelerate the evolution of PR in law firms, taking the PR function to new levels. These will include the following:

- The international and domestic trend for law firm consolidation is likely to increase. Firms will be encouraged to improve their PR to make them more attractive to possible suitors. This is particularly important for rankings in the legal directories.
- Instances of in-house law PR functions working with a firm's lawyers to advise a client on media relations will become more common. This will become especially true in litigation, where disputes are often driven by a wish to safeguard a client's reputation.
- Law firms that want to attract investment from outside the partnership by listing or by accepting private equity investment will be driven to enhance and protect their reputation.
- As firms seek to distinguish themselves by their sector and industry knowledge, the ability to be public advocates for their client's agenda will become increasingly important. The best lawyers will seek to influence the law as well as to interpret it.

Given these factors, legal PR in the next decade will concern the profile of law firms being valued and realised. Whether large or small, firms that adopt a more positive approach to working with the media will reap significant benefits.

The role of governance and CSR in the success of a legal practice

Corinne Staves
Richard Turnor
Emma-Jane Weider
Maurice Turnor Gardner LLP

1. Introduction

How do some law firms make it all look so easy?

The most successful clients insist on using such firms despite their relatively high charges. Their comments on the issues of the day are eagerly sought. Their published profits per equity partner are the envy of other firms. They attract the brightest and best lateral hires and trainees, many of whom go on to great careers as partners in the firm. Even those who leave use their former connection with the firm as a mark of distinction.

Such success is achieved only through years of carefully directed effort. Effective governance is crucial, but increasingly, a socially responsible approach to business is also proving essential.

2. Defining success

Different stakeholders, both present and future, look for different qualities in a law firm.

2.1 Partners

Partners look for fulfilling careers in an environment that enables them to achieve their full professional potential. They expect to be rewarded accordingly.

Profitability, and especially profits per equity partner (PEP), is commonly used to measure relative performance. However, more thoughtful partners will regard sustainable profitability and growth in both good and bad times as a more important measure than short-term PEP.

Partners also hope to be able to carry out interesting and varied work with highly successful clients, and to be part of a team that enjoys recognition among clients and competition alike. Most will also hope to work in a supportive environment and to achieve a reasonable work-life balance.

2.2 Outside investors

Both Australia and now England and Wales allow outside investors in law firms. These investors' aspirations often overlap with those of the partners. However, their interests may also diverge, especially in relation to how the firm is to be managed and how its profits are to be shared.

2.3 Clients

A firm's financial strength and the adequacy of its insurance cover are important, but clients judge a firm primarily by its quality and value.

General reputation is a crucial badge of quality. Without that, a firm has to work much harder to convince existing and potential clients. Reputation is won through involvement with the most prestigious clients and by demonstrably leading thought in key areas of interest.

Of course, technical expertise, competence and experience are essential components of quality. However, a firm's understanding of a client's business and market, its attention to a client's interests, its responsiveness and accessibility, its ability to deploy teams with an appropriate mix of experience, its commercial approach to opportunity and risk and its capacity for innovation will tend to be the deciding factors.

Clients want to know that the firm's priorities are aligned with their own. Law firms therefore need to devote time and resources to understanding their clients' businesses and ensuring that they always identify with the client. This can be demonstrated by the way in which work is delivered and staff and partners interact with clients, as well as more formally through pitch processes, panel applications and the like.

Clients insist that their legal advisers should provide value for money. This does not mean that clients necessarily want the cheapest advice. Rather, firms should provide greater value, taking into account the cost, than their competitors. Quality is an essential component of value. Increasingly, clients insist on cost certainty and expect their advisers to be able to plan and manage projects to budget, as well as offering innovative charging arrangements.

Finally, clients increasingly expect to see firms espouse best practice in areas such as equality of opportunity and community-related activities.

2.4 Staff

Of course, staff expect to be remunerated at a competitive level that reflects their contribution and commitment. However, this is only part of the package.

The quality and variety of work, and the opportunity to work with a highly regarded team, are important. So too is a challenging and interesting workload that will equip them for their future careers and give them experience that is likely to be valued by future clients and employers. Fee-earning staff value the prospect of a fulfilling long-term career with the firm. They also look for recognition and appreciation, a collaborative and supportive atmosphere, equality of opportunity, quality of training and a good work-life balance. Many are also attracted by a firm's socially responsible approach and the opportunity to be involved in pro bono or community projects.

2.5 Suppliers

Suppliers prefer to be associated with a firm that is financially robust and well managed, and that has a reputation for being socially responsible and fair in its dealings.

2.6 Community

The wider community in which a law firm operates is also a stakeholder. It expects the firm to uphold the rule of law, to facilitate access to justice, to operate fairly, to provide equality of opportunity and to operate sustainably. Society also looks to the legal profession as a whole to provide services at little or no cost to those who cannot obtain legal advice otherwise.

2.7 Regulators

Finally, the firm's regulator is likely to share many of the concerns of clients and of the community as a whole. It will be most concerned about those issues that affect the fundamental principles of the profession, such as access to justice, the rule of law, integrity and independence. It will also be concerned about those issues that might adversely affect clients. For example, does the firm have systems in place to safeguard client money? Does it keep clients informed about legal costs and the risks associated with their transactions and disputes? Do its staff and partners have the necessary professional qualifications, expertise and experience? Does the firm have adequate professional indemnity insurance?

However, regulators are increasingly likely to intervene more generally in the way that firms are managed and organised. In England and Wales, for example, the Code of Conduct of the Solicitors Regulation Authority (SRA) requires firms to apply sound business and risk management principles.

If a firm is to achieve its full potential in the eyes of all these stakeholders, it needs to operate in a way that promotes their interests. If its strategy and the way it does business are aligned with the interests of stakeholders, especially its clients, the firm can achieve genuine success.

This is likely to be achieved only through effective governance.

3. The elements of effective governance

3.1 Vision and strategy

If a firm is to develop a sound strategy that will enable it to succeed in changing times, it first needs:

- an understanding of the environment in which it and its present and future clients must operate and how this may change;
- the foresight to appreciate the potential impact of those changes on it and its clients; and
- a clear view of the kind of services it wishes to provide and to whom, both now and in the future.

From this vision the firm can develop a broad strategy that focuses on the needs of its chosen clients, thus contributing to their success, and on providing exciting and rewarding careers to its partners and staff. The strategy should be dynamic and capable of responding to change. It may incorporate measurable milestones or goals to which the firm can aspire and that it can use to measure its success.

The challenge is to focus the efforts of everyone in the firm behind the strategy.

Everyone needs to understand their own part in achieving the firm's goals and to play it with skill and enthusiasm.

3.2 Culture and values

The firm needs an internal environment that will enable it to attract and retain the best lawyers, and to deploy them to the greatest benefit of its clients.

This deployment will be far more effective if there is a culture of collaboration, in which individuals put the interests of clients, the firm and the team before their personal interests. All members of the firm must understand and apply its values (including client focus, hard work, mutual support and respect, equal opportunities and a culture of lifelong learning) in everything they do. Achieving this requires leadership, communication and training. The firm's performance evaluation and appraisal process will be an invaluable tool.

3.3 Leadership, reporting lines, oversight and accountability

A firm needs to be able to adapt to change. It therefore needs a robust management structure and clear reporting lines so that management can provide well-informed and timely direction and guidance. Everyone in the firm should understand who reports to them and to whom they have to report, as well as their roles as both leaders and followers. This will ensure the rapid flow of information and ideas up and down the organisation.

The best decisions are made through the interplay of ideas between individuals with differing points of view and experience. A formal forum, such as a partners' conference, is an ideal opportunity to share ideas and to build the firm's sense of identity and purpose. It can also stimulate innovation, especially in firms that are large and have a disparate group of disciplines, perhaps all over the world. Similar sessions with fee earners and support staff can also be valuable, although from a practical point of view these may need to be limited to local discussions.

Everyone in the firm should be accountable to and mentored by someone else, so that all decisions are taken responsibly and in the light of fully informed discussion. Even the senior management team should be accountable to an oversight body, such as a firm council, a full board or committee, or to the partnership as a whole, in order to reassure partners and staff that they are acting in the firm's interests.

Until now, oversight bodies have generally included respected partners who are not involved in management. Such independent partners can provide assurance that management is acting in the interests of the firm and its partners, but they do not provide access to the experience and ideas of anyone who has worked outside the firm, let alone outside the profession. There is a danger that the firm will simply carry on as it always has without realising that it, or the wider profession, could be doing better. Where permitted by the relevant regulator, a firm may be able to achieve a competitive advantage by involving non-executive directors with wider experience, especially in other professions or with experience on the boards of companies operating in client markets.

The oversight body itself should be accountable to the firm and its partners. This can be achieved through an electoral process, perhaps supported by an appointments committee comprising members of the oversight body who are independent of the management. Ideally, the elections will take place by secret ballot under independent supervision and through an appropriate polling system such as the single transferable vote.

3.4 Performance management

A robust system of performance management will help to focus everyone's efforts on the firm's clients and strategy.

The appraisal process will involve the gathering and sharing of evidence about an individual's past performance, in the form of financial and other data, and all-round feedback. This will be followed by a discussion of how the individual and his or her team should contribute to the firm's strategy and goals in the ensuing period. The discussion should be constructive and should encourage the person concerned to come up with his or her own ideas. Concrete and measurable objectives should be agreed for the next appraisal period.

The appraisal process is often used to inform decisions about remuneration. However, in order to avoid cluttering the appraisal discussion with remuneration issues, the appraisal report should ideally be used as evidence to justify remuneration by someone other than the appraiser.

3.5 Risk and opportunity management

The effective management of risk is an essential part of governance. Indeed, in England and Wales the SRA requires all firms to have effective systems and processes in place to manage risk.

Firms need to anticipate anything that might prevent them from achieving their goals. Systems should be put in place to monitor and control those risks in a proportionate way. Categories of risk might include:

- those associated with clients or with competitors;
- risks arising from changes in market conditions;
- internal financial risks, risks arising in relation to partners and staff and their training and supervision; and
- risks that might mean that the firm is regarded as non-compliant by its regulator(s).

The firm's culture should encourage the identification and management of risks. It is impossible to eliminate risk altogether, but it is possible to put in place safeguards so that the firm can seize opportunities without unacceptable risk.

The system must be able to distinguish those risks that merit attention at the highest level from less pressing issues, so that proportionate arrangements to manage each risk can be made at an appropriate level. This means that risks must be graded according to both likelihood and impact.

Clear reporting lines and responsibilities are integral to any risk management process. Each risk area should be monitored by a nominated team or individual who should report to the management at appropriate intervals, at times of particular danger and as a standing item under the usual board or committee cycle.

An effective risk register that identifies risks, the controls in place, those responsible for monitoring and managing risks, and any gaps in control is an invaluable way to ensure that everyone is aware of the risks for which they are responsible and of what they need to do to control them. It also ensures that management keeps all key areas of risk under appropriate review.

3.6 Internal and external audit

Many firms, and all firms in England and Wales that operate as companies or limited liability partnerships, have to undertake an external audit. The auditors are, of course, concerned with risk and its control as well as financial results.

More and more larger firms also have their own dedicated risk management and internal audit function. Internal auditors assure the partners that appropriate controls are in place for monitoring risk and recommend improvements in accordance with best practice. Smaller firms may ask external auditors to provide this service. Firms that do so can gain the benefit of an auditor's wider knowledge and experience. They may be able to measure their own practices and performance against those of other firms.

Firms in England and Wales will in future be required to appoint two compliance officers. In particular, all firms will have to appoint a lawyer as their compliance officer for legal practice (COLP). This person will be responsible for ensuring that the firm has the required systems and processes for recording breaches and notifying them to the regulator. A compliance officer for finance and administration will be responsible for ensuring the adequacy of processes in relation to client money (but not, perhaps strangely, for wider finance and administration issues, which fall to the COLP).

3.7 Policies and working practices

A firm's policies and standard working practices will be important in guiding partners and staff in how to conduct themselves in their day-to-day professional activities. They can be used to create a contractual commitment to comply with the firm's governance processes. Topics to be covered by these policies might include diversity and equality of opportunity, business acceptance, client complaints and what to do in the event of an interruption in business continuity.

Policies must be clear and accessible, and perhaps made available to all staff via an intranet site. All team members, and especially new ones, should receive training on key policies. Members of the firm can be asked to evaluate their understanding of the policies regularly, thus identifying any gaps and enabling appropriately targeted training to be arranged.

3.8 Capture, analysis and use of management information

Client complaints are a key performance indicator. The most enlightened firms will want to record any occasions on which they have underperformed, and to use this information to learn and improve how they do business. It is important to create a culture in which people are prepared to disclose their own mistakes, without fear of blame and punishment. In this way potential areas of risk can be identified and appropriate steps taken to address them through training or other safeguards.

Requesting and acting upon client feedback, and peer reviewing files selected randomly and according to risk, are other useful ways of collecting vital information about quality and failures of best practice.

The new SRA Handbook, which came into effect on October 6 2011, provides that proper records and analysis of complaints, along with systems to ensure quality of service, are required.

4. Corporate social responsibility

4.1 An increasing focus on corporate social responsibility

Business is no longer simply about profitability. Law firms, like any other business, have to view corporate social responsibility (CSR) as an integral part of what they do if they intend to compete in the modern world. The principle of CSR may also be seen as the basis of building a sustainable and responsible business.

The approach of each firm to CSR will be unique, but the following tenets are generally regarded as key:

- equality and diversity;
- ethical standards of behaviour, by both the firm in general and each employee;
- preserving the environment; and
- community work, such as pro bono and charitable activities.

Effective CSR initiatives are increasingly important to how stakeholders view a firm's success.

4.2 Embracing equality and diversity – examples from the United Kingdom

Regulators are increasingly interested in equal opportunities. There have been several recent regulatory developments in the United Kingdom.

The Equality Act 2010 harmonises and simplifies the rules against discrimination. It details what a business can and cannot do in relation to its partners and staff. Much of the act came into force on October 1 2010. Under Section 158, employers can take proportionate measures to enable or encourage the participation of disadvantaged or under-represented individuals. Section 159 goes further and permits the more favourable treatment of people from a disadvantaged or under-represented group when it comes to recruitment or promotion, provided that they are equally qualified. This section is highly controversial and has not yet been brought into force, but it offers an insight into likely future attitudes and approaches.

The new SRA Code of Conduct includes a core obligation to run the business or carry out one's role in a way that encourages equality of opportunity and respect for diversity in how businesses are run or roles are carried out. This is coupled with additional mandatory outcomes, including an obligation to monitor actively and respond to issues identified by the firm's equality and diversity policy, and to update protocols as appropriate. Staff and partners must be made aware of this policy and act in compliance with it. The policy must also be made available to clients and the SRA upon request.

Some may see this legal and regulatory framework as a burden that conflicts with their commercial interests. However, the reverse is true. The legal profession has recently been criticised for not being diverse enough and not giving those from less privileged backgrounds access to the profession. A perception of exclusivity can damage a business. It will diminish not only the pool of talent from which a firm can recruit, but also the pool of potential clients.

A firm which does not benefit from a broad range of different perceptions and experiences is likely to be less innovative. Ensuring diversity and equality allows a firm to enhance its ability to act in the best interests of its clients – and clients themselves are increasingly becoming more diverse.

Despite the legal and regulatory environment and the strong business case for equality and diversity, the editor's introduction to the UK's *Lawyer Magazine*'s Diversity Report of 2010 paints a rather depressing picture. It states, for example, that:

- class and education remain fundamental determinants of entry into the profession;
- women are greatly under-represented at senior levels;
- black and minority ethnic lawyers are often paid less than their peer group; and
- gay and lesbian lawyers often suffer discrimination.

Until Section 159 of the Equality Act 2010 comes into force, UK firms can do little to promote an under-represented group, since doing so is likely to discriminate against another well-represented group. However, part of the problem is governance. Someone needs to be responsible for keeping equality and diversity under review. In July 2011 the UK Legal Services Board approved guidance requiring regulators, law firms and chambers to measure and publish indications of diversity and social mobility in the legal workforce. Some firms have already published this data on their websites and this is a step in the right direction.

Firms can also look for and nurture talent in individuals from diverse backgrounds. Student mentoring schemes, for example, may be an excellent opportunity to build links with less privileged students and their schools. At the same time, such schemes might also fit well with CSR programmes. Firms might also broaden their selection criteria to permit a wider mix of recruits.

Clients are generally ahead of their legal advisers in appreciating the importance of diversity, and many major corporate and financial clients take into account a firm's approach to diversity when appointing panel firms or considering pitches.

4.3 Ethical standards of behaviour

Ethical behaviour is especially valued by clients, staff, regulators and society as a whole.

Ethical standards tend to be set by the behaviour of the individuals at the top of the organisation. Senior individuals have a responsibility to establish a clear and positively principled climate. This then permeates down through the organisation.

The costs involved in adopting and rigorously enforcing high ethical standards are far outweighed by the benefits, especially in terms of reputation and client relationships. Clients are unwilling to compromise their own ethical standards through association with any business, let alone a legal adviser, that does not subscribe to the same ethical code as them. Failure to integrate socially responsible behaviour into a firm's core values can be very damaging to its corporate image and brand. Indeed, the Enron debacle led to the worldwide demise of Arthur Andersen.

Failure to adopt ethical standards can have other serious implications. Signatories to the 1997 Organisation for Economic Cooperation and Development Anti-bribery Convention have committed to put in place legislation to criminalise the act of bribing foreign officials. In the United Kingdom, for example, this has given rise to the Bribery Act 2010, which takes a hard line on corrupt behaviour in business and criminalises some aspects of corporate behaviour, such as improper financial inducements. The increased attention to corruption in business is also reflected in the SRA's new Code of Conduct, which includes a set of core principles for ensuring that firms are compliant with the SRA's own ethical stance.

4.4 Preserving the environment

CSR also encompasses the preservation, restoration and improvement of the environment, not least because running a large business itself has a substantial environmental impact. There are a range of regulatory, reputational and financial reasons to pursue an environmentally responsible business strategy.

Clients and staff increasingly expect to see energy and power-saving devices in the workplace, and effective recycling policies.

It has long been known that something as simple as switching off the office lights at night is socially responsible, but many firms now have a more comprehensive approach to reducing their carbon footprint. In the United Kingdom, this commitment to reducing carbon emissions has been a mandatory requirement since the introduction of the CRC Energy Efficiency Scheme (the CRC, previously known as the Carbon Reduction Commitment Scheme) in April 2010. The CRC covers all organisations that use more than 6,000 megawatt-hours per year of electricity (equivalent to an annual electricity bill of about £500,000). While this mandatory requirement may not apply to many law firms, it will certainly apply to many clients. Climate change and the reduction of emissions are therefore firmly on the environmental agenda for the foreseeable future.

In the United Kingdom, the Legal Sector Alliance includes representatives from 220 law firms that are working together to take action on climate change by reducing their carbon footprint and adopting environmentally sustainable practices. The 20 executive members of this alliance have publicly committed to cut carbon emissions and thus to drive change in the legal sector.

Paperless filing systems are far more efficient and encourage waste reduction. The most sophisticated firms have devices in place to monitor the entire heat output of a building and 'recycle air' to ensure the greatest efficiency possible. Some firms also educate their staff appropriately so as to ensure that there is collective responsibility for a firm's environmental impact.

A number of companies have successfully built their business around environmental considerations. Law firms can emulate this, thus aligning themselves with their clients' own environmental goals, securing client and staff loyalty and playing a wider role in promoting the preservation of the environment among their clients.

4.5 Community work

In major cities such as London, some of the biggest firms are based right next to some of the poorest areas and can play a role in helping to develop cohesive communities. Engaging in community outreach projects and pro bono work not only helps wider society and fulfils a key tenet of CSR philosophy, but also benefits the firm itself. Working with less advantaged sections of society can show a firm's human face and can generate good publicity. In addition, encouraging employees to engage with the community through volunteer work can motivate them and help them to feel that they are making a contribution both to society and to the firm itself. Such outreach work can also develop employees' valuable interpersonal and team-working skills, which will benefit the firm and its clients. In some firms, community work has now become so central that fee earners have target hours for pro bono activities each year. Meeting these targets is considered as part of a merit-based remuneration package.

The legal profession has long struggled with the perception that it is closed to people from disadvantaged backgrounds. By engaging with local communities, firms can help to counter this impression and ensure that talent is able to emerge from areas that might otherwise have been overlooked.

Law firms can also cement client relationships by participating in community activities that have been espoused by the client or by inviting the client to participate in the firm's initiatives. Such an approach emphasises the firm's belief in the underlying importance of CSR and its alignment with what is important to the client.

4.6 Core values

CSR demands that firms move beyond mere legal compliance by integrating socially responsible behaviour into their core values and recognising the business advantages of doing so. If a firm fails to do this, then its future as a trusted adviser to its clients is likely to be undermined. CSR can help a firm to win new business, to increase client retention and to develop and enhance relationships with clients. On top of this, environmental policies can reduce operating costs.

5. An increasingly complex world

Governance and CSR are not made any easier by the increasing complexity and scale of legal practices, and the environment in which they operate.

Size creates its own problems, especially for firms that operate from multiple locations in many different business areas. Different business areas and geographies may command different levels of profitability and require different business models. This leads to stresses. A matrix of systems is often needed to cope with business lines that also cut across geographical regions.

The changing regulatory landscape is also having an effect. As noted above, in England and Wales, outside investors are to be permitted, and this will pose new governance challenges as firms work out how to preserve their independence while benefiting from investors' own management expertise and how to share their profits.

Globalisation multiplies these complexities, as firms struggle to cope with multiple tax jurisdictions and regulators. A more complex structure is often implemented to achieve optimal tax and regulatory treatment overall, but complexity makes governance more difficult. At the same time, firms have to adapt to different markets and clients with different cultures, and different attitudes to social responsibility.

These factors all pose new challenges, but if a firm is clear about its core values and its global strategy and uses effective governance structures and processes, it should be well placed to overcome those challenges.

Women and the business of law

Lynn M McGrade
Borden Ladner Gervais LLP

1. Introduction

Recently, while attending the annual meeting of the International Bar Association, I had occasion to speak to one of the managing partners of a law firm in Austria. I asked him what issues were of most concern for his firm's management, as I was curious to know how his priorities compared with those at our Canadian firm. Certainly the global recession and business development were issues. However, he also noted that retaining women was a key issue for management. On the basis of this discussion, and many others like it, it is clear that if you are in law firm management today, it is very likely that the issue of retaining and advancing women in your firm is important.

Retaining women in private practice is not only a key issue for law firm management, but also one to which there are no easy answers. While women have been graduating from law schools in approximately equal numbers as men for more than 20 years, the number of women in partnership and leadership roles in law firms is dismal. In Ontario, only 21% of partners of law firms are women.[1] Among the largest law firms in the United States, only 15% of equity partners are women.[2] In terms of leadership, 11% of large US law firms have no women on their highest governing committee and 35% have only one woman on this committee.[3]

2. The business case for retaining and advancing women

These statistics are not new. In fact, the percentages of women partners in firms have remained fairly static for about the last 20 years.[4] So why is the retention of women in law firms suddenly gaining so much attention from law firm management? Because it is good for business. Those firms that can provide an environment in which women can excel and become leaders will be more successful in the business of law. Why is this the case? Consider the following:

- Women represent a valuable intellectual resource. Many of the women that graduate from law schools at the top levels of their classes are hired by law firms. The firms that can retain this resource will be able to provide a higher level of professional excellence and expertise to their clients.

---

1 Law Society of Upper Canada, *Career Advancement into Partnership: Law Firm Guide* (Toronto: Law Society of Upper Canada, Ontario, 2011), p 4.
2 National Association of Women Lawyers and The NAWL Foundation, *Report of the Sixth Annual National Survey on Retention and Promotion of Women in Law Firms* (Chicago: The National Association of Women Lawyers and The NAWL Foundation, October 2011), p 3.
3 *Ibid*, p 4.
4 *Ibid*, p 3

- Studies have repeatedly shown that diverse teams produce better results.[5] Generally, a woman's approach to problem solving and the consideration of an issue is different from a man's. The result of combining these approaches is that more options may be considered and/or combined, with a greater chance of achieving the best result.

- More and more large clients are demanding diversity in their legal teams. Our firm has seen a significant increase in the number of requests for proposals with questions that relate to diversity in general and the representation of women in particular. In the United States in 2004, a group of general counsel at large companies launched a movement known as 'A Call to Action'. This aimed to affirm a commitment to diversity in the legal profession among those general counsel. A similar initiative is underway in Canada. It is certainly no longer appropriate for a firm to send a team of all-white men to pitch for a work mandate of substance. Clients are actively looking for diversity on teams. Firms that can attract and retain strong women who can join and lead client teams will have a clear advantage in pitches to clients in the future.

- The number of women who are in a position to award legal work to law firms is increasing. While these women will not exclusively award work to women professionals, they will have a lower level of gender bias (discussed further below) and some may have a higher comfort level or 'fit' with another woman professional.

- Ensuring that your firm cultivates an environment in which women can thrive and excel is the right thing to do. More and more men, both at firms and with clients, have wives and daughters who are engaged in professional careers. A firm that does not work hard to address issues that create barriers for women professionals will not be viewed favourably by those who respect the role and rights of the woman professional.

3. Steps that firms should take

While much has been written on the many positive steps that law firms can take to enhance the retention and advancement of women in their firms there are three that I believe warrant special attention. These are tone at the top, business development support and gender bias mitigation.

3.1 Tone from the top

To achieve an environment that fosters woman professionals, it is critically important for a firm's management to communicate and champion the importance of women as a business imperative. This goal should be incorporated as part of a firm's strategic plan and its mission statement, and regularly presented as a business priority in the meetings of management and partners.

As noted above, there is a strong business case for firms to ensure that woman professionals can thrive and excel. Management must continually reinforce this business case and the resulting importance of this business imperative. Highlighting

---

5   Catalyst Inc, *Why Diversity Matters* (New York: Catalyst Information Centre, November 2 2010).

the issue in a firm's strategic plan will help to ensure that it is a point of focus for key management decisions and processes, such as leadership appointments, partnership admission, practice group strategic planning and resource deployment. It will also ensure that proper measurement tracking[6] and accountability are devoted to the matter. This is key because organisations have a much better chance of achieving their strategic goals if progress is measured.

Measurement can be particularly helpful to attaining strategic objectives when it is combined with transparency. Transparency with lawyers about what is being measured and what has been found keeps management accountable and actively focused on improving the numbers day by day. Perhaps more significantly, it will also reinforce the importance of management including the issue in their annual/strategic planning process. Transparency sends a strong message to the firm (and its women lawyers) that management considers the issue important.

3.2 Supporting business development

Success in a law firm is largely defined by the number and value of the client relationships that each lawyer brings to the firm. Those lawyers who have the largest client bases, and are the notable rainmakers, are viewed as successful and powerful. Ultimately, they will tend to become the firm's leaders. For those firms that want to ensure that women can thrive and excel and ultimately assume leadership positions, a focus on ensuring that women have adequate business development support and training is key.

All too often, it comes as a surprise to woman professionals that they need to have developed independent client relationships to excel at a firm. Women associates often assume the role of dutiful and hardworking associate to a senior partner to the detriment of their own business development. A recent study by the National Association of Women Lawyers found that many large US firms had no women in their lists of top 10 rainmakers.[7] Firms (and women lawyers) must address this issue as a priority.

Here are some suggestions for firms to consider:

- Be clear about the importance of business development to a lawyer's success from the beginning of his or her practice. Young lawyers often receive a clear message from their firms about the importance of billable hours, and that salaries and bonuses are derived from these. Realising the importance and significance of business development comes at a later stage. Often it is too late to establish the foundations and good habits of business development. Consider implementing a tracking system that rewards and encourages business development initiatives at the same (or an even higher) level of prominence as billable hours.

---

6   The Law Society of Upper Canada has produced an excellent guide for firms wishing to maintain gender data. See Law Society of Upper Canada, *Gender Collection Guide for Law Firms* (Toronto: Law Society of Upper Canada, Ontario, October 2010).

7   National Association of Women Lawyers and the NAWL Foundation, *Report of the Fifth Annual National Survey on Retention and Promotion of Women in Law Firms* (Chicago: The National Association of Women Lawyers and the NAWL Foundation, October, 2010).

- Offer strong business development training programmes for young lawyers. The concepts of client development and marketing are not usually taught at law school. Accordingly, well-managed firms provide extensive business development training to lawyers. While this type of training is critical for both women and men, it is important for firms to recognise that women lawyers may benefit from some specialised training. There are a number of reasons for this. They include a lack of suitable role models and exclusion from male networks. I am often asked by young women lawyers, "How do I, as a 30-year-old woman, invite a 50-year-old male client or prospective client out to lunch?" Questions like this are good ones. Their answers often depend on the particular circumstances at hand, and these can be analysed and discussed in women-focused training initiatives.[8]
- Firms should not make the mistake of focusing extensively on women-to-women business development for its women lawyers. Although the number of women who are in a position to award legal work to law firms is increasing, the vast majority of work directed to a firm still comes from men. It is therefore critical that women lawyers are trained for all situations of business development.
- Implement a strong career development programme. This includes developing good templates for helping young lawyers to focus on business development. It also involves a system of accountability and mentorship so that young lawyers can seek input and guidance on the appropriateness of their plan and how effective they have been in implementing it.
- Consider offering specialised business development support for certain lawyers. A firm may find that some of its lawyers are exceptional technical practitioners, but are failing to develop their business side. Other lawyers may put a lot of time and initiative into business development, but to little effect. In these cases, it may be appropriate for firms to invest in targeted resources. These might include one-to-one coaching from an external business development coach. Some accounting firms have been very successful at implementing sponsorship programmes.[9] In these, a successful rainmaker or powerful firm leader is assigned a lawyer as a special one-to-one coaching project, and so helps him or her to meet the requirements for admission to partnership.

Business development support and training is relevant for all lawyers at a firm, not just women. As a result, the proposals above make equal sense for both men and women. However, firms that incorporate the unique business development challenges faced by woman lawyers into their programmes and training will have more successful results. As women often represent a large percentage of younger

---

8   The American Bar Association Women Rainmakers of the ABA Law Practice Management Section has produced a good reference book on women's business development. *Women Rainmakers' Best Marketing Tips*, Theda C Snyder, Third Edition.

9   Catalyst has produced an excellent report on sponsorship in the context of women. See Catalyst Inc, *Sponsoring Women to Success* (New York: Catalyst Information Centre, August 2011).

lawyers, it stands to reason that a business development programme that resonates with their circumstances will be more effective. Putting in place the tools to ensure that young women lawyers become successful marketers is an important factor in retaining and advancing women, because effective business development is a key component of success, and ultimately of leadership within a firm.

3.3   Mitigating gender bias

The final area that should be a focus for law firm managers is the initiation of programmes to reduce the impact of gender bias on woman lawyers. Gender bias is unconscious. It is the outward result of feeling comfortable with those who are most similar to ourselves. For women, it can mean being viewed as less dedicated (because of family commitments, whether real or perceived), lucky (as opposed to competent) or difficult (where a man might be viewed as forceful or confident). Gender bias is likely one explanation for why law firms are often referred to as the 'old boys' club'.

In seeking to mitigate the impact of gender bias on women lawyers, firms might consider the following steps:

- Ensure that management is aware of the business reasons for advancing women and is educated on gender bias and its impact on advancement. For example, as part of the partnership admission process, the relevant decision makers should review the firm's mandate and gender data statistics, and ensure that all decisions are made with this information in the front of their minds.
- Performance questionnaires, partnership admission criteria and other tools used by the firm to measure success and advancement should be scrutinised for gender neutrality.[10] Often questionnaires and criteria such as this are filled with terms that are associated with stereotypical male-based leadership characteristics, such as 'action oriented' and 'driven'. Effective leadership characteristics that are more commonly associated with women, such as 'collaborative' and 'team based', are given little or no weight.
- Install diversity training programmes for all lawyers at the firm. Management in particular should undergo this training at least annually. Practice group leaders also need to be trained, as they play a critical role in advancing and retaining women in their groups.

As we become more diverse as a society, we will become more diverse as a profession. With that greater social and cultural diversity, more challenges will come into play and the complexity of retaining and advancing women will become even more pronounced. Firms that focus in earnest on the challenges and rewards of diversity will gain a competitive advantage as the business case for diversity continues to grow.

---

10   An excellent resource for this purpose was produced by Catalyst. See Catalyst Inc, *Cascading Gender Biases, Compounding Effects: An Assessment of Talent Management Systems* (New York: Catalyst Information Center, 2009).

Being successful within your jurisdiction

Philip Rodney
Burness LLP

There is a view that legal firms can be successful in the current environment only if they are global or international in scale. If you are not a behemoth, the theory goes, you must resign yourself to the scraps under the table.

Certainly, it is striking that of the top 10 of the *Legal Business* 100 2011, six are global elite firms and two are major international firms, along with one major UK firm and one major City firm.

But are the big firms necessarily the best-performing ones? Possibly the true measure of efficiency is the profit that a firm makes per lawyer. When we look at those figures instead, we find a top 10 comprised of four global elite firms, three major City firms, two London mid-sized firms and one Scottish firm. Of the 10 firms with the highest turnover, only four feature in the top 10 in terms of profit per lawyer.

What this demonstrates is that in terms of financial efficiency, there is not just one formula for success. Certainly, one does not have to be a global player in order to succeed.

1. Background: Burness LLP and the Scottish legal environment

Although Scotland is part of the United Kingdom, it is in many respects separate from that of England, Wales and Northern Ireland. It has partial self-government and its own legal system. Its population is around 5.2 million, with a gross domestic product of about £140 billion. Its major industries are financial services, energy, whisky, electronics, tourism and creative industries. Its major trading partners are (in descending order) the United States, the Netherlands, Germany, France, Spain, Ireland, Switzerland, Belgium, Italy and Singapore. There are roughly 8,500 solicitors in private practice in Scotland. It is a small jurisdiction – it is often said that you can be bicoastal with offices just 40 miles apart!

Burness was founded as W & J Burness WS by two brothers around 150 years ago. It was initially a full service firm with an office in Edinburgh. A former partner, who joined in the 1960s, told me that at that time it was regarded as a parvenu firm – that is, it was not part of the establishment.

The following story illustrates that culture. A former senior partner of the firm was having lunch around this time in one of Edinburgh's most celebrated clubs. His opposite number in one of the then more established firms said, "I see that you have just appointed the son of a fish and chip shop owner as a partner in your firm. We only appoint gentlemen as partners." To which the response from my predecessor was apparently, "That's interesting. In Burness, we only appoint lawyers as partners."

Being slightly outside the establishment has given the firm energy and ambition. It has also attracted a certain type of person – committed, driven and with something to prove. Its culture has always been diverse and inclusive. It has a balance of home-grown talent and lateral hires.

In the early 1980s a small office was established in Glasgow and in 1990 another in the Channel Islands, on Guernsey.

In 1998, some strategic decisions were taken that materially affected the firm's direction. The firm had both a successful commercial core and a vibrant private practice. However, the two businesses were very different, with distinctive aspirations. The combination of the two also sent a confused message to the market.

As a result, it was decided that we would focus solely on commercial work. The firm's private client team (and the Guernsey office) demerged amicably and successfully. The remaining commercial wing then merged with a successful boutique practice in Glasgow, Alexander Stone & Co. (It is from here that I joined.) This effectively doubled the size of our Glasgow office. To mark the change, the firm dropped the 'W & J', becoming just Burness, moved to new offices in Edinburgh and worked hard at projecting its commercial focus.

2. Creating a new strategy and a new brand

When I was appointed chairman in 2005, we carried out a strategic review, analysing what had been achieved over the previous seven or eight years. I spent a lot of time on the diagnosis phase, speaking to clients and partners. In the two months following my appointment, I also tried to meet everyone who worked in the firm.

A number of things were clear. First, we were successful. We had a talented partnership with some recognised market leaders. Our staff retention was high and we had a good name in the market. What was missing, however, was a clear or accepted direction. There was no consistent view as to which part of the market we occupied. Some saw us as mid-market. Others were more aspirational. There was a sense that we occupied any given part of the market almost by accident.

Second, partners had had to develop their own individual practices. Individual parts of the business operated in their own silos. There was a feeling that we were a number of different businesses operating under a common brand. Our financial performance was average. We were certainly not one of the most prosperous firms.

My conclusion was that while we had the potential to be a lot more successful, we had to decide whether we were happy with our lot or whether we aspired for more. If we did have higher aspirations, what was our goal and how were we going to achieve it?

Starting from first principles, it was clear from speaking to clients that we had a very talented team of lawyers. That was an excellent starting point.

After extended internal debate and discussions with an outside consultant, we identified four objectives:

- to be regarded as a premier law firm, focusing on quality not price. We wanted to be distinct, not just one of a number of players in the market. This meant improving our service delivery and fine-tuning every part of the process. We also needed to improve our profile;

- to focus initially on being regarded as leaders in corporate finance, banking, commercial property, dispute resolution, employment, construction and projects. This did not mean that we were abandoning other service lines. It meant, however, that they would be regarded at that stage as supporting roles. This caused some disquiet in the minds of those whose practices were in these areas. We had to demonstrate that the firm would benefit if we concentrated on developing in phased stages. This was just an early phase;
- to achieve profitability at the top end of the market. Not only would this benefit existing partners, it was also essential for ensuring we recruited and retained the most talented teams in the future; and
- not to open an office in London, unlike our competitors. This was an important point in our strategy. It meant that at that stage in our development, we would not add offices beyond our jurisdiction. This was for a number of reasons:
  - We could concentrate our resources on our objectives without the distraction of operating elsewhere.
  - We understood our market, had expertise in Scottish law and could reasonably aspire to be the best commercial law firm in Scotland. If we were to open in London, we would be only bit players in that market.
  - Given the disparity of overheads between operating offices in Scotland and London, we would avoid tensions within the partnership.
  - Importantly, we would not be seen as competing with London and other English law firms for business, and could further develop referral relationships with them.

When we adopted that strategy, it seemed controversial. Many firms were opening in London. However, we judged that the market was not right for us.

Some partners wondered why we needed to make any changes at all, given that the firm was successful. But by and large, everyone was happy. We now had to implement a strategy that was uncompromisingly about being the best in our jurisdiction.

First of all, we needed a management structure that allowed us to make quick and effective decisions. It also had to create checks and balances. In response, we created a two-board structure. Our operations board, comprising our managing partner, heads of department, director of finance and HR director – was responsible for the day-to-day running of the firm. The second board was responsible for governance and strategy. By splitting the functions, we ensured that strategy was always on the agenda and not something that was debated only if there was enough time.

We invested heavily in our training, IT and client database systems. We sought to improve every element of our work.

In our market research we asked clients what they liked about us and what they thought could be improved. One always embarks on research like this with some trepidation. However, the responses were mostly very positive and included the folowing:

- Clients that instructed us knew that they would get advice, not disclaimers;
- Clients knew that if they instructed on something at 6:00pm on a Friday, the work produced would be on their desk at 9:00am on the Monday – and on

budget; and

- People found us easy and fun to work with (surprisingly, they found some of our competitors 'high maintenance').

The most negative response was that we were backwards in coming forwards. We were reticent about asking for the next piece of work. We thought it was genteel reserve, but some clients saw it as aloofness.

We also asked clients, "If Burness were a car, what brand would it be?" The most popular response was Audi, followed by Volvo. We had seen ourselves more like a BMW. We were also surprised at how low our brand recognition was.

We set about addressing these issues. A programme of regular client reviews was established. These were conducted by me, as chairman, and our marketing director. It was important that clients were able to speak openly to us rather than to the relationship partner. All feedback was recorded and acted upon. During these reviews, we found that clients knew less about the range of services we provided than we expected. They were keen to know more about the firm. And they made a number of useful suggestions.

We then formed a client advisory group and invited representatives of major clients and suppliers to join. The idea was to meet over lunch three times a year to test ideas with our users and discuss market conditions. Those clients who participated really liked this.

The next task was to increase our profile, and we did this in a few ways. We talked to the media. We opened up about the firm. The first time that an article was published about our success, we were worried as to how our clients would react. The response was entirely positive. Our clients wanted to be associated with successful advisers. Partners started to comment to the media on issues of importance. Some wrote articles. A number of them became recognised as thought leaders.

Finally, we invested in our brand. The catalyst for this was one client review. This client scored us 11 out of 10 for everything. At the end of the discussion, he described Burness as "the best-kept secret in Scotland". He meant it as a compliment. But it underlined that while we were excelling at what we did, we still were not visible enough in the market.

In developing our brand strategy, we decided not to go to an agency with previous experience of working with a professional services firm. Instead, we engaged the Leith Agency, which had famously been responsible for the iconic Barr's Irn Bru campaign. It had a sense of fun and pizzazz.

After some focus sessions with our partners and clients, we identified our brand values: style, ambition, innovation and passion. Our rebrand was not just to do with a logo. It was about the way we talked to the market. It was about how we projected ourselves. We were *Vanity Fair* rather than *Scottish Field*; Missoni rather than Holiday Inn.

Our new brand identity was launched to favourable feedback. Unusually, there were articles about it in both of the Scottish quality broadsheets.

In developing our brand strategy, we anticipated the importance of social media. We now use Twitter, LinkedIn and regular blogging to promote what we are doing.

3. Achieving success

It would be wrong of me to judge the success or otherwise of our particular strategy. What I can do is point to the following outcomes in a difficult market:

- Our market share has increased;
- We have achieved an above-average net income growth;
- Our profitability has been consistently high;
- Our partner remuneration is among the highest in the market; and
- We have enjoyed an increased profile in our market.

In 2012, Burness LLP is a purely commercial law firm with offices of equal size in Edinburgh and Glasgow. We have around 150 lawyers, with 250 people in total.

There have inevitably been major challenges along the way. We have seen a major recession and cross-border firms competing in the market. But we have managed to grow the business, despite being based only in one jurisdiction – and a small one at that.

Why is this the case? There are many reasons, but the following in particular have been very important:

- understanding our market;
- dealing with issues of scale and reach;
- exploiting our size and independence; and
- raising our profile.

There is no magic formula, and these are not the only issues that one needs to consider. But they are factors that we believe should be addressed if one is to succeed in one's own market.

3.1 Understand your market

It is true of all businesses (not just law firms) that you need to understand not only what you are going to sell, but also to whom you are going to sell it. The 'if we build it, they will come' approach is a risky one. Just because you are highly skilled in an area of law does not mean that there are clients who will be prepared to buy these services. For example, only a finite number of clients will buy aviation law services.

The safer approach is to look at your market, understand its key sectors and identify what legal services are required now and are likely to be needed in the future. This necessitates reading the economy, studying sector activity and properly understanding how the businesses of your clients or potential clients will develop over the short, medium and long term. As David Maister, arguably the guru of law firm management, once said in a lecture, "Lawyers should read fewer law journals and more trade magazines."

One advantage of operating in a comparatively small jurisdiction is that it is easier to understand your market. You are closer to it. Being part of the fabric of a jurisdiction rather than an outsider with an interest in it can be a great benefit.

One often sees firms from other jurisdictions attempting to understand a local market without success. Their disadvantage is that they they do not live in the market. One picks up a lot about the market through osmosis – going to football matches on a Saturday, attending dinners on a Thursday night, being on the board of a local institution and generally being part of a local network.

A desktop analysis of a local market may give you an understanding of some of its parameters. But it will not give you the touch, feel and smell of the environment, which is the key to success in a small jurisdiction. Being close to one's market allows an intimacy that a global player may not have. It allows one to understand and engage with what is happening at a local level. We sometimes see general counsel in large corporations preferring to engage local firms rather than UK or global firms with a small market presence because they better understand the nuances of the market.

Also, without sounding too parochial, many of our local clients like working with Scottish firms. Although some of our competitors like to market themselves as UK firms, we are proud of being Scottish. That does not mean that we do not get involved with business beyond our boundaries, however.

3.2   Dealing with issues of scale and reach

Operating in a single jurisdiction also means that you have to understand your limitations and work with them. It is said that a strategy is not really a strategy unless you are prepared to lose clients. However, with the right strategy it should be possible to deal with international transactions even though your home base is in only one jurisdiction.

Even firms operating in just one country increasingly need to deal with cross-border issues. If you are not prepared to handle international work, you will preclude yourself from a substantial and profitable part of the market. Without offices in other jurisdictions, how do you deal with such transactions? One aspect of succeeding in a single jurisdiction is creating a network that will provide global reach. It is too late to wait for one of these transactions to come along before you create that network. It has to be in place in anticipation and as part of your overall strategy.

Sometimes the international dimension to a transaction or case will require you just to refer your client to a foreign firm. On other occasions you may have to work in partnership with a firm in another jurisdiction. In still further instances, you may need to project-manage teams of lawyers in other firms and jurisdictions. In each situation you must have complete confidence in the firms you are working with. Little creates more bad will than involving another firm that lets your client down. There is no point in saying to your client that the other firm is to blame for any error or unsatisfactory performance. As far as the client is concerned, it is the responsibility of the host firm as it made the introduction.

So how does one create a virtual network? How does one ensure a consistency in other jurisdictions with which the client will be comfortable?

The first issue is to identify the countries in which cover is likely to be required. One has to recognise that it is impossible to ensure cover in every jurisdiction. Having identified the geographic umbrella that you need, the next step is to identify the range of specialist expertise that is likely to be required. Is it likely to be corporate support, tax, litigation, environmental and so on?

Once these parameters have been mapped, a number of approaches can be taken.

One of these is to look at the international law directories. They will give an indication of the rankings of law firms and individual lawyers in various jurisdictions. What they do not provide, however, is an understanding of what they will be like to work with. They do not indicate a firm's style and approach and how it might coincide with yours – and therefore the standards that your client has come to expect.

The second approach is to join an alliance. The benefit here is access to a ready-made network. The principal disadvantage is that within that network there is not always a consistency of expertise and service delivery. Only by getting to know the members of the network through regular attendance at conferences and the like can one really have the confidence to work with its members. Another disadvantage might be the obligation to cross-refer business within the network, which might preclude other opportunities to develop relationships with other foreign law firms. If one does join an alliance, it is crucial to meet the firms in the jurisdictions to which you are most likely to refer business and ascertain whether they are of a suitable calibre.

An alternative to joining an alliance is to use the network of a global firm. The advantages are the same as joining a network. The elements are the same too. Just because the firm's head office has an excellent reputation does not mean that, say, its Milan office will be as good. Again, you have to test the overall quality.

Finally, one can build up one's own network. This can be done through attending conferences such as those arranged by the International Bar Association, the American Bar Association and so on. The advantage of this is that it allows you to examine the goods for yourself and be selective. One can get a much clearer understanding of the law firm that one is dealing with and its approach and, in the process, create referral opportunities.

In practice, a mixture of these approaches will be required. In my experience, few things will upset a client more than being referred to a firm that does not match your own ability and approach. While cross-referral opportunities are to be encouraged, it is more important to be satisfied that the service that your client will receive will match what they are used to than to look for the possibility of reciprocation.

3.3   Exploiting your size and independence

There are definitely some advantages to having a multi-jurisdictional organisation. Scale, increased geographical cover and brand recognition are three positive elements.

On the other hand, a large firm with offices in many jurisdictions will be unable to make and implement decisions as swiftly. Our size means that we can adapt quickly to our market.

As an example, in the downturn of 2007-8, Burness was in a position to make swift decisions about the correct size of the firm and could take steps quickly to implement them through consultation. As a result, we were able to establish a recovery pattern the following year. Other, larger, firms took much longer to react and turn around their performance.

Partners in a single jurisdiction firm are also likely to present a more uniform approach without the tensions of market factors in competing jurisdictions. In our firm, the partners can all sit around one table – albeit a large one.

Again, if we want to embark on a new venture, the timeframe for analysis, consultation and implementation is much quicker. Competing jurisdictions and vested interests will not get in the way.

3.4 Raising your profile

In a smaller jurisdiction, you not only get closer to your market, but are part of that market. Being an insider allows you to be involved to a greater extent with your client base compared with a multi-jurisdictional law firm headquartered in London, for example. You can understand the nuances of the market and focus a lot more clearly.

You can also get closer to the media and speak to the opinion formers. A smaller market brings you closer to the business issues being debated and on which you can more readily comment. This enables you to establish a stronger profile.

We often see situations in which our client has been involved in a transaction in the public domain and we have an opportunity to provide an overview or perspective. This can lead to media coverage and members of the team being identified as leaders in particular sectors.

Scale has its advantages, but being indigenous and close to your market has benefits too. At the end of the day, there is no one recipe for success – just be great at whatever you do!

Building a leading position in a regional firm in Central and Southeastern Europe

Horst Ebhardt
Wolf Theiss

1. Introduction

In less than 15 years, Wolf Theiss has developed from a small Austrian law firm into one of the leading regional firms in Central and Southeastern Europe (CEE/SEE). The Wolf Theiss story is that of a small first-generation firm with visionary founders, not bound by traditions or limited by an established market position like its Austrian competitors. It is also the story of a group of entrepreneurial young partners who seized upon the serendipitous sudden emergence of a large marketplace on their doorstep, and had the vision and collective will to build the firm into a regional powerhouse.

In addition to telling the Wolf Theiss story, I touch upon some of the main challenges facing a law firm that has decided to expand internationally and describe how we addressed these challenges at Wolf Theiss.

2. The beginnings

Every firm has a specific history and background that provides a unique behavioural framework and shapes its later evolution. This background can create a conservative environment. It can provide stability, but can sometimes also lead to restrictive or overly cautious behaviour. A firm's history can also give it a dynamic personality, encouraging initiative and facilitating ambitious growth when external factors are favourable. Wolf Theiss falls into this latter category. We can see today that its particular starting position was essential to its later success.

Wolf Theiss was founded in 1957. For many years it remained a small but highly regarded firm in the conservative and fragmented Vienna legal market. In 1994 the two named partners, Peter Karl Wolf and Andreas Theiss, decided that they wanted to build a larger, market-leading firm. The only way to grow quickly at that time was to make lateral hires. Unlike many competing firms, where the partners focused on short-term profitability or on funding their retirement programmes, Wolf and Theiss sought to create a new and highly attractive platform for young and ambitious partners. The essential features of this new platform are still the core of the firm's DNA and constitute the essential bases for its success:

- a truly entrepreneurial environment;
- a focus on quality;
- generous financial arrangements; and
- an egalitarian structure.

To attract the type of young partners they wanted, Wolf and Theiss offered relatively generous and motivating financial conditions and gave the new partners a significant voice in how the firm was run. For the Vienna market in the mid-1990s, which was 20 to 30 years behind the US and UK legal markets, this was an unprecedented innovation. Other firms were convinced that such a model for expansion would not work and that by giving up control Wolf and Theiss were putting themselves and their firm at risk. The strategy was indeed not without risks. But by choosing this path, Wolf Theiss was able to attract a core of highly motivated, entrepreneurial young partners.

Many of these lawyers were already marked as the next generation for the dominant local firms. However, they felt unable to achieve their ambitious goals for practice development in the hierarchical environments of those firms. Most had significant international experience and had worked for major international law firms or organisations earlier in their careers. Most felt that the Austrian firms they were with before joining Wolf Theiss were not keeping up with international standards and that they were unwilling to change. The firms generally did not have a one-firm mentality, since most operated as relatively loose groupings of sole practitioners who mostly looked to the overarching 'firm' for cost synergies. Our influence on our respective firms' strategies was limited and often perceived as a threat or challenge to the institution rather than a welcome and proactive input. In contrast to those other firms, operating in what we saw as a complacent, slow and backward legal market, Wolf Theiss had the clear goal of becoming a new leader with the ambition to grow aggressively.

After joining Wolf Theiss, we helped to fine-tune a strategy for growth. We looked at the models of successful US and UK firms and sought to create a new firm along similar lines. The essential elements of our strategic vision included:

- a non-hierarchical platform;
- a democratic decision-making environment;
- a high degree (by Austrian standards) of legal specialisation;
- a culture of client service; and
- a focus on quality legal services that met high-end international standards.

These ingredients may sound obvious today, but at that time it was not a combination that could be found in any of the existing Austrian law firms. From the perspective of the local Austrian market in the mid-1990s, Wolf Theiss was a somewhat revolutionary concept. It was met by strong scepticism and a clear rebuff from the established firms. Suddenly we were the new kids on the block and, because of our aggressive growth strategy, we were not particularly well liked by the establishment. The psychology of being something new, however, had a wonderfully uniting effect on the group. It created a strong 'can-do' mentality and the spirit of togetherness that drives start-up companies.

Looking at the broader context, it is clear that this new type of firm (new from a local perspective) was created at just the right time, in response to a market that needed a higher standard of service and as part of the broader professional evolution of the European legal services market. The platform we set up was not only the basis for building a market-leading firm in Austria, but also a strong base for our later international growth strategy.

3. The beginning of our international expansion – goal and strategy

In the mid-1990s, the partners of Wolf Theiss were becoming increasingly aware of the tremendous opportunities available in the new markets that were emerging in Central and Southeastern Europe. The CEE/SEE region was a unique opportunity: a largely untapped new market with significant growth potential. Accordingly, in 1997 we began to revise our growth strategy to focus not only on Austria, but also on the wider CEE/SEE region.

A number of factors influenced our decision to seek to grow into a regional law firm. These became the core drivers of our new growth strategy.

3.1 New regional markets

The markets in CEE/SEE, some of which border Austria, were opening up after decades of Communist rule. They were attracting large amounts of foreign direct investment. Vienna had long been an entry point for eastward investment, even during the Cold War, and was developing into a regional hub for international companies that wanted to expand into CEE/SEE. Many of these companies established regional headquarters in Vienna due to its proximity to these markets. Austrian companies and financial institutions were also expanding into these new markets with the goal of becoming regional leaders. Two of Wolf Theiss's banking clients grew in just 10 years from purely local banks, with perhaps 5,000 personnel in Austria, to dominant regional banks with staff of 50,000 throughout the region. Vienna became a financial and organisational centre for investments in CEE/SEE, expanding far beyond its previous role as the capital of a small country. Although that regionalisation was well underway by 1997, we thought that we still had a good chance to capture a share of the legal market.

3.2 Inactive Austrian firms

No Austrian law firms yet had a significant presence in this newly emerging region. Consequently, Austrian blue-chip companies were unable to use their regular outside firms when doing business in CEE/SEE. We saw this as an opportunity to attract as clients the major Austrian and international companies and financial institutions that were expanding in the region. Few high-quality law firms were pursuing a regional strategy in CEE/SEE, although a few North American and UK firms had set up offices in several countries to try to capture major transactional work. Our goal was to create not only a transactional capability, but also a full service firm that would become the first choice for investors coming into the region. We would do this by providing a service tailored to the needs of those clients. Our goal was to be perceived as, and to become, a region-wide specialist.

3.3 International and local support needed

The international firms active in the region worked primarily on large-scale transactions involving the privatisation of state assets. They had their own teams of international transactional lawyers, and generally relied on local law firms only for country-specific advice. The local law firms were thought not to have the experience needed to run international transactions by themselves. In our view, the complexities of emerging markets, and the rapidly evolving and changing legal systems, required more than just flying in a team of experts with the backing of an unrelated team of local lawyers. Our goal was to become a long-term regional player by providing a service that could handle all types of major transaction, but also addressing the ongoing needs of companies and banks in transitional economies. By 1997, many international firms were scaling back or even closing their CEE/SEE offices, as the first wave of privatisations ended. We therefore saw an opportunity to match UK/US offerings (service quality, capability to do international transactional work), while at the same time providing local expertise for both transactional and non-transactional work, and to do so through a network of offices across the region.

3.4 Enlarging our home market

We decided to expand our small home market of Austria to the larger regional market of the CEE/SEE region at a moment when that latter market had just started to take shape. An exceptional historical opportunity allowed us to target that region during a phase when it was undergoing rapid growth. In other words, we created a new and much larger home market by defining the CEE/SEE region as our new strategic 'home'. For much of the first decade of the 21st century, the CEE/SEE economy was the second-fastest growing in the world. The region's legal market was still largely untapped and there were no law firms with long-lasting client relationships rooted in the region. We were therefore able to move into this expanded home market with clients which had also begun to expand in the region. On many occasions we were able to build lasting new client relationships or significantly deepen existing relationships by moving into this large new market in this way.

3.5 One firm, one level of quality

In the 1990s the legal market in CEE/SEE was still fragmented. Local law firms had only existed for a few years, and although they often had good lawyers they generally lacked the experience or commercial understanding expected by sophisticated international clients. Many international firms, including some of our Austrian competitors, chose to cooperate with local firms, rather than establish their own offices. We felt that the proper way to become a significant regional player was to combine international experience and local depth, and to offer that combination consistently across all of our offices. We saw this 'one-firm' strategy as the only way to guarantee a consistently high level of service and quality in all jurisdictions where we operate. That strategy was at the core of our thinking. Consistently achieving that level of service would require a significant financial investment over many years, but such an investment was essential if we were to build a superior regional firm.

3.6 Regional expansion

As newcomers in Austria, we had to come up with a bold strategy if we were to compete successfully and win high-profile clients. At that time, we had only a limited institutional client base and our regional expansion provided the means to develop relationships with international companies coming to the region. Other Austrian firms were reluctant to expand internationally and were not prepared to make the investments necessary to achieve such roll-out in a sustainable manner. We therefore saw a chance to attract major new Austrian clients which were expanding regionally and had to seek separate counsel for their work in CEE/SEE. With no Austrian firms serving the CEE/SEE region, they had started to turn to major US and UK law firms for help. Given the opportunity to work with an Austrian firm with local expertise and offices, many of these companies turned to us. Our assistance to these clients on important CEE/SEE transactions allowed us to build close relationships. These have significantly boosted our growth within Austria and in the rest of CEE/SEE.

3.7 Working with global and leading law firms

Due to the limited legal services available in the newly emerging CEE/SEE region, there was great potential for providing global law firms and their clients with services. Wolf Theiss was convinced that by offering high-quality services, we could assist major law firms from around the world. Most of these did not expect to become active in CEE/SEE, and were relieved that they could rely on us to support them and their clients in the region. We were happy to offer our services as local counsel to premier global and national law firms, while honouring their existing relationships with their clients. We also saw this local counsel role as a way to acquire know-how, stay abreast of global legal developments and learn from state-of-the-art legal practices in major financial centres, and to apply this in CEE/SEE. This strategy has worked well and we continue to partner with leading legal practices, now mostly in a position of co-counsel, on projects and transactions across the region.

3.8 Specialisation and market leadership

Finally, we had the simple ambition to build a new and better firm, and to break out of the traditionalist Austrian market. From the outset we wanted to become the leading legal practice in Austria and CEE/SEE in terms of both market position and involvement in top-end legal work. To us, 'leading' means holding a top three position in every market in which we operate. We also needed to achieve greater firm-wide specialisation in those practice areas where we wanted to achieve a market-leading position, including gradually expanding that specialisation to all countries where we operate. This inevitably meant building a critical mass in the core practice areas and making specialisation a cornerstone of our strategy. We knew that this would take several years. Our goal was to achieve gradually a high-quality standing in each of our core practices and across all our offices.

While we had these clear goals and an ambitious overall strategy, we did not have a precise action plan, investment budget or schedule for achieving them. In 1997, we knew only that we needed to open up offices in new markets; to build, export or acquire know-how; to acquire significant clients and to construct a regional network of offices.

Based on our experience gained over the years, we would not undertake such a major project today in the same way or with the same 'start-up' mentality. Looking also at the recently turbulent markets, we would now be more careful and spend more time preparing business plans, budgets and stress tests to ensure that we got the economics right and, at the same, that we were in a position to compete immediately for high-end work. But this does not mean that we were not careful in how we managed our expansion. In line with our strategic consensus, we were prepared to take entrepreneurial risks. We did not expect immediate or precisely defined financial returns. The goal of becoming a leading regional firm in terms of quality and client profile took precedence over the wish to achieve defined profitability levels. Although high profitability was, of course, a medium-term goal, as a start-up company we were fully aware of the fact that achieving quality and market recognition had to come first, and that our project would take years to reach its goal.

Not only did we share a strong entrepreneurial spirit; we were also in absolute agreement about the need to make decisions based on long-term goals, rather than short-term results, and to invest in the firm for the long term. This meant that we had the right mindset for a young and aspiring firm and, perhaps, the ideal mindset for any firm that has the ambition to become a successful international firm. For profitable local law firms considering international expansion, the costs associated with a roll-out can have a negative impact on profitability in the medium term. But we were different. Our lack of high profitability at the start meant that we did not focus so much on the risks of expansion as at the opportunities it might bring. In that sense, we were in a fortunate situation.

Looking at all this with some distance, and leaving aside the 'hard' ingredients that make up a strategy, I can say that there was a certain attitude of generosity among the partners – and in particular the two founding partners – that drove many of the firm's decisions and created a good overall atmosphere. That may sound imprudent or even amateurish. However, reflecting on our history and what mattered most, this intangible value created a strong bond and sense of harmony among the partners. This attitude attracted additional strong lateral partners who could not find a comparable entrepreneurial and dynamic base at that time. We thus started out as an ideal platform, combining – perhaps only by chance – several key ingredients for exceptional growth:

- a strong vision;
- strong ambition and commitment to realise the vision;
- the necessary talent;
- a collective long-term mindset;
- a sense of sharing and collaboration;
- tolerance and generosity; and
- an exceptional market opportunity.

This may almost sound like propaganda. What I am trying to say, however, is not that everything at Wolf Theiss was or is perfect and simple (or that we did not make mistakes), but that the firm started out with a united platform of shared core values that somehow created the soul and spirit of the firm. And this spirit, combined with a unique historical opportunity, was essential in driving the firm's success.

4. Opening new offices

Between 1998 and 2008 we opened 11 new offices in the CEE/SEE region. In 1997 we had 25 lawyers, and today we have 325 lawyers serving a market of over 135 million people. Our revenues grew on average by 19% per year from 1997 to 2010. We are now a leading regional law firm and the largest law firm in Austria, ranked Tier 1 in all practice areas. We have come a long way in implementing our strategy, although we know that this process never ends and that the fast-changing legal market will always require changes and refinements.

I would now like to describe some of the factors that influenced our development, our experience with some of the challenges of a growing firm and certain lessons we have learned. Those lessons will not apply to every firm, but may be helpful in addressing and evaluating similar issues in the process of expansion.

5. Technique of expansion ('greenfield' versus merger)

One of the most difficult decisions when opening a new office is how to go about it. The firm needs to minimise the financial risk while ensuring that it is able to compete effectively in the new market as soon as possible. The decision is even more difficult in a mature and competitive market, since opening such an office will undoubtedly require a greater initial investment. The decision often involves strategic pressure to accommodate the wishes and expectations of important clients. Or it may involve capturing market share or extending global coverage, or expanding a key practice area or core industry coverage.

As a result of our situation in 1997, we did not feel such outside pressures. We were able to define freely the nature and speed of our own expansion. This freedom has changed over the years as we have achieved market standing, and we now service clients throughout the region. We can no longer afford not to be able to support clients with a high level of quality from day one. In many ways we are now an international law firm with exactly the same challenges as other international firms, and we again will have to learn how best to cope.

In 1997 we took an opportunistic approach and decided to open our first foreign office in Prague. The Czech Republic has been one of the most successful emerging economies in CEE/SEE. It was a logical first step for Wolf Theiss, since several of our clients were already active in that country. In addition, I had spent four years working in Prague in the early 1990s for a US law firm. When I joined Wolf Theiss in 1997, one of my principal tasks was to help the firm to open its Prague office. This we did in 1998.

We decided on a 'greenfield' roll-out, bringing on board local attorneys. We asked one of our young Austrian partners to relocate to Prague to ensure the full integration of the new office. We felt that this would help to build a one-firm mentality as well as provide our clients with German-language support and a sense of familiarity. This approach was slow and cautious, but it worked well for us, thanks to the high quality of Czech lawyers who joined us and the team-leader capabilities of the Austrian partner who headed the Prague office for its first five years. In 1999 we recruited a partner of Czech nationality who was educated at a US law school and had worked for several years at a major New York law firm. This significantly enhanced our international transaction capabilities in Prague. In wanting to recruit this partner, we were in competition with a major international law firm. We succeeded because we could offer both a new platform and entrepreneurial space to shape an office and a practice.

Prague exemplified the good combination of seconding a home-grown partner to a new office and bringing lateral teams on board. We used a similar model for almost all of our subsequent office openings. However, if we were to undergo the same expansion today, we would first try to merge with a leading local law firm and so acquire a going concern. In 1997 this was not possible, because we did not know the market players and were not able to identify a suitable firm as a merger candidate. We also lacked the experience of bringing on board and integrating another firm and, as a relative unknown, would have had difficulty in convincing an established firm to merge with us.

We opened almost all of our other offices through similar methods. Typically, we would send one of our Austrian partners to set up a new office or we would hire lateral partners. We undoubtedly benefited from the cultural proximity and historical ties of Austria to the countries in the region and the regional diaspora that lives in Austria. Our Serbian office, for example, was set up in 2002 by one of our young partners who, though raised and educated in Austria, is of Serbian descent and agreed happily to relocate to Belgrade. Our office in Slovenia was set up by a young Austrian partner whose mother came originally from Slovenia and who is a native speaker of Slovenian.

In Bucharest, we brought on board a US-qualified partner with a decade of on-the-ground experience in Romania. In Sofia, we recruited a UK-qualified partner who had lived and worked for many years in Bulgaria. Both of these partners were well equipped, through their strong local business and legal connections, to build strong local teams of lawyers and help develop local client bases for the firm.

In Slovakia, Croatia, Bosnia and Herzegovina and Ukraine, we recruited teams of local lawyers and provided support primarily from Vienna. In Croatia and Bosnia and Herzegovina we eventually brought on board US partners from leading international law firms to coach, train and develop our local partners and lawyers, and help them to acquire skills in operating an office and running complex transactions.

In two markets we followed a different model. In Albania, we acquired the entire Tirana office of a magic circle firm that had decided to leave that market in 2004. This was the one occasion where we responded to an opportunity presented to acquire a local practice, rather than planning an opening based on a perceived need.

In Hungary, we faced a different set of issues. The country is geographically close to Austria and is of significant interest for many of our Austrian and international clients. We had long felt that this was a market in which we needed to be. It was also, like Prague, a market that by the middle of the first decade after 2000 was highly developed, with strong local firms competing with the established offices of international firms. The competition was fierce. Entering this market on a greenfield basis would have been extremely difficult; a Budapest office would need to be relatively large and sophisticated from the beginning in order to service and attract clients. A merger was seen as the best alternative. However, partners in local law firms were generally quite content with their existing arrangements and saw no economic or lifestyle benefit to joining an international firm.

In 2007 we were lucky to find a large team of high-quality Hungarian lawyers who had built up one of the leading energy practices in the region. They had decided to leave the magic circle firm where they had practised for many years, and were delighted to join Wolf Theiss. The firm's regional platform was ideal for them to service their existing energy clients, which were active throughout CEE/SEE. For Wolf Theiss, it was also an ideal fit. The Hungarian practice was not only self-sustaining, of high quality and able to provide a full service offering from day one; it also provided a strong platform for building a much stronger, firm-wide energy practice.

The process of opening the various offices therefore occurred in different ways, depending on the individuals and teams available. Every partner who joined us had an entrepreneurial attitude and was looking for a new and dynamic platform where he or she could expand his or her practice. They all shared the vision of building high-quality legal practices in the environment of a newly emerging and ambitious international firm.

Many of the partners who joined the firm had worked for US or UK-based international firms. These firms had broad international strategies, but in many cases the CEE/SEE region was at most an afterthought. This often made it difficult for these partners to push through, or simply get approval for, innovative plans for their practices or offices. At Wolf Theiss, the CEE/SEE region was the home market, and these partners had no difficulty in making their colleagues understand their local needs and concerns. The firm's regional strategy therefore enabled it to recruit high-quality international transactional lawyers who were committed to the region.

We were usually able to get to know the local legal markets well before we actually moved in and opened our own offices. Due to the close relationships we had developed with Austria's leading banks and other large international clients active in the region, we worked for many years on transactions in various CEE/SEE countries before we set up offices in those countries. During these transactions we worked with many local law firms and identified the most highly regarded lawyers. Working with them as local counsel, we already had a high level of familiarity with the members of the teams once they joined us. This helped us to avoid difficult situations faced by other firms, which had not done sufficient due diligence on lateral hire candidates. As a consequence, we have lost very few partners and have maintained a continuity in our practice growth that is absolutely vital to our success. This stability has made it easier for Wolf Theiss to move beyond pure geographic expansion and to develop integrated international practices and firm-wide areas of specialisation.

6.   Leadership and office management

There is no ideal recipe for how to open an international office. One feature is key, however: the quality of the local leadership team. It must be able to integrate with the rest of the firm, motivate its local lawyers and, of course, service sophisticated clients.

Running the office of an ambitious law firm that has the goal of becoming a top-three local firm is a demanding position. It requires a huge commitment of time and effort both from firm management and from the individual who assumes the role. These individuals are key to building the institutional fabric of a firm and instilling loyalty and trust in their younger colleagues. Integration and motivation are essential to the development of good young lawyers and to keeping them happy within the firm over the long term.

The lawyers who head the local offices must possess specific skills. They must be not only ambassadors for the firm to the outside world, but also the representatives of their local colleagues with respect to the main office. They must ensure that the firm's goals are met and its policies are adopted locally. At the same time, they need to adapt those policies to local conditions and ensure that suitable conditions are in place for meeting the firm's goals. It is essential that the partners who are to lead offices can manage and motivate people, have strong interpersonal skills and can act as role models. That is, that they can manage an office in the best sense of the word.

It is not so important whether a firm grows by way of mergers or by acquiring teams or seconding partners. Each method has its own specific advantages and potential drawbacks. Having the local office headed by the head of the local firm that has merged with the parent firm, for example, can lead to a lack of loyalty or sense of belonging to the newly merged entity. The culture of the local office often remains that of the firm before it merged, rather than that of the new entity. Conversely, seconding a partner from the head office may make local lawyers feel that they are not viewed as equal partners, able to manage their own affairs. With these issues in mind, we have applied specific criteria for bringing on board new partners or seconding partners to new offices. Possessing top legal skills is, of course, of great importance, but having the skills to manage people and an office is equally important. The two sets of skills are not mutually exclusive, but they are not always found in equal parts within the same individual.

Making the right choice of office head is essential. Mistakes can lead to enormous problems and can tie up the entire management of the firm far away from home base.

Finding the right people and getting them to join can take a long time and a lot of patience. They must be well integrated into the overall firm and its practices, while leaving room for a certain local freedom and individuality. In other words, management must find someone who can not only take responsibility for the office, but also maintain ambitious one-firm standards. That can be a fine balance, and a successful firm will put a lot of emphasis on maintaining that equilibrium. This in turn means that the firm's management must maintain close contact with its office heads and work hard to create an atmosphere of support, trust, understanding and personal respect. Like any relationship, this requires close dialogue, a clear schedule of personal interaction, the sharing of information, transparency and involving people and giving them a proper say.

This rule should apply at all levels and among all partners of a firm – after all, this builds the fundamentals of a firm's culture and holds it together. But maintaining that quality of relationship with the heads of offices in a multi-country law firm is a distinct feature. It is the only way to bridge cultural differences, and to create acceptance of and appreciation for the cultural differences that may require different solutions in different markets. Those cultural differences will always exist and the firm must accommodate them if it wants to maintain harmony, even at the expense of uniformity.

To make the local lawyers feel that they are equal participants in the firm and not just statistics for the head office, it is essential for a regional firm to take its diversity seriously and to cultivate its inter-office relationships on a regular basis. This is a decisive element in attracting and keeping top talent and supporting an entrepreneurial spirit.

7.   Practice area coverage and practice integration

A cornerstone of our growth strategy has been to create regional practices that are tightly integrated. This means that we can provide a true one-quality service offering across the region. This has required a significant investment over many years, but it has been essential for building a leading regional practice.

Our strategy was to become a leading regional firm in the following areas:

- corporate and M&A;
- banking and finance;
- real estate;
- litigation and arbitration;
- labour and employment;
- tax;
- intellectual property;
- regulatory and public procurement; and
- competition and antitrust.

In support of that strategy, we created firm-wide practice groups for each of these practice areas. Each lawyer joins one primary practice group as a full member. Many of our lawyers are also adjunct members of one or two additional practice groups – in particular, lawyers in smaller offices that still need a more general mix of practices. Each practice group has its own firm-wide leader. The practice groups are responsible for training and for building know-how and sharing it across all offices, as well as for marketing the practice.

In addition to regular practice group meetings held by telephone, all members of the practice groups firm-wide, including junior lawyers, meet in person twice a year. This personal contact has been essential for building up integrated practices of people who really know each other well and are used to working together. It also helps to promote a firm-wide culture, which is important to maintaining relations within the firm. Getting everyone in the practice group together is costly, but for Wolf Theiss it is manageable thanks to the geographical proximity of our offices. This close personal interaction on a regular basis has helped us to rapidly develop firm-wide know-how. It also allows us to respond to the needs of our clients in a structured and state-of-the-art manner.

Client feedback shows that our service offers the same standards across the firm. Achieving such alignment of quality between offices has enabled us increasingly to win clients that want a firm that can provide services and consistent quality throughout the region. In my experience, clients know whether an international firm is actually capable of offering the same quality across multiple offices or whether this is just a marketing slogan.

Our focus on a firm-wide deployment of such specialised areas of practice as intellectual property, employment, tax and competition has shown real benefits. Specialist law firms and specialised departments within general practice firms that want high-quality legal support in CEE/SEE now retain us to help them to address their clients' needs throughout the region.

Investing in developing practice groups and training programmes to maintain firm-wide quality is likely to affect a firm's short-term profitability. But it will also secure its long-term success. In addition, young lawyers looking to join a law firm will want to see that a firm is willing to invest in their future. This is perhaps particularly true for lawyers in countries with less developed legal markets, where the training offered by local firms is inadequate for servicing international clients. A proper firm-wide training programme is therefore essential for attracting these young lawyers, who are of course the future of any firm.

8. Compensation, lock-step and diversity

In order to attract the best and brightest lawyers, a firm needs to offer compensation at the highest level of the markets it is in. It needs to pay these rates even before it reaches the level of profitability that actually covers such compensation levels. Offering high-quality training and development opportunities can, in part and for a limited time, substitute for a high compensation level, but eventually the compensation will need to be at market rates. I believe that this applies to any legal marketplace.

For a regional law firm, the goal in setting compensation must be to achieve a pay scale that takes into account market (ie, country-by-country) differences, but ensures the integration and satisfaction of its lawyer group as a whole. This is a difficult process and the results need to be monitored constantly and adjusted when necessary. Our approach has been to offer our lawyers attractive levels of compensation in accordance with local standards, but to align compensation across all offices as soon as similar levels of relative productivity are achieved. In case of doubt, we have taken the more generous approach and eliminated or reduced compensation differences. Overall, our policy has been to offer equal compensation for equal performance.

The ability to provide an international service offering is a key asset that differentiates an international law firm from many of its local competitors. For a regional firm such as Wolf Theiss, which attracts many of its clients based on its ability to offer same-quality services in all of its offices, it may be necessary to invest disproportionately in some offices in order to achieve the desired level of service. For example, it may be necessary for a time to pay market-level salaries in order to attract the capable lawyers needed to provide the level of service expected, even if the current workflow does not justify such high salaries. This can create internal conflicts and disputes, but it should be viewed as a form of long-term investment necessary to secure a high-quality service even before an office has fully conquered its market and achieved the desired level of profitability. The ability to offer regional capabilities benefits the entire firm, enabling partners in different offices to secure clients that they would otherwise be unable to bring on board. That benefit is difficult to measure, but it is of paramount importance and it should be shared – financially – by all partners.

Achieving a partner compensation system that pleases everyone is impossible in any firm, but it is perhaps especially difficult in one where the level of revenues per lawyer and profitability per office can vary tremendously, depending upon the specific factors of various markets. It is difficult to maintain a standard set of billing rates that works well in countries with economies as different as, say, Austria and Albania. Since our work is primarily for international businesses, rather than for local clients, and is a result of our very large investment in know-how and specialisation, we manage this problem pretty well. However, the different economic circumstances of the different countries in which we operate inevitably affect the profitability of the various offices and lawyers.

In order to achieve maximum integration and equality, we have chosen to use a firm-wide, two-tier partner system. This system applies in the same way to all offices. Equity partners of the firm, wherever they are based, are part of the same lock-step. Salaried partners have the same base compensation and a performance-based component that depends on their overall contribution (and not just financial contribution) to the firm. Irrespective of whether a firm has a lock-step system or a more merit-oriented system, the partnership must ensure that the overall benefits of the firm are shared and that short-term indicators do not overrule the longer-term need to achieve maximum integration and cohesion. A more generous approach that does not over-emphasise temporary differences between profit centres will, in my view, secure the long-term success of an international law firm.

9.   Conclusion

Setting up a network of international offices is a huge undertaking for any firm. Its success depends on a number of competing factors, not all of which are within the firm's control.

Wolf Theiss was fortunate to come of age at a time and in a place in which the factors for success were all present or could be created. The firm also benefited tremendously from a unique set of circumstances, with the sudden emergence on its doorstep of a huge and growing market. Nevertheless, its success has been achieved through a shared sense of vision and undertaking by the partners, through careful planning, and through hard work.

As an established international firm, Wolf Theiss now faces new challenges. Our continuing success will depend on how well we are able to institutionalise our original spirit and adjust our strategy to meet the demands of an ever-changing and increasingly competitive environment.

Going global: aligning local and global priorities

Robert Millard
Linklaters LLP
Carole Silver
Professor of Law, Indiana University Maurer School of Law

1. Introduction

The globalisation of business and finance has arguably been the defining characteristic of the world's economy over the past quarter century. Like other professional service providers, lawyers have had to adapt in order to maintain their currency. Moreover, the world's economic and socio-political shifts, coupled with changes in client demands that have emerged since the global economic crisis began in 2008, increase the pressures for change. In response to these challenges, lawyers and their firms must develop strategies that navigate a multitude of regulatory and market forces, both at home and abroad.

At a minimum, responding to globalisation may require no more than a shift in mindset that allows lawyers to develop sensitivity to differences in legal framework, negotiation strategies, languages, professional norms and roles. For many, this may be adequate. For those seeking to capture the rewards of globalisation more directly, this list is merely a foundation for action. That action may include:

- physically growing outside their home countries; developing alliances and networks; and
- adopting new organisational structures and new approaches to client service, including educating clients unaccustomed to sophisticated legal services in the kinds of services that international law firms can offer and why the value they deliver might (or might not) be worth the fees they charge.

In this chapter, we consider several drivers of and challenges to international growth for law firms. We begin by briefly outlining the early trends in international growth, focusing on the forces that lead firms to grow outside their home markets and their approaches to such development. Next, we turn to the organisational structures that firms use to cope with the challenges of internationalisation and the ways in which regulatory regimes influence these choices. The chapter then turns to strategic decisions relating to global growth. Finally, we discuss the ways in which law firms might address the tensions between local realities that affect individual offices and their desire to maintain a cohesive, profitable organisation at the global level.

2. A brief history of the international growth of law firms

International offices are nothing new for law firms. US-based law firms have been active outside the United States since 1922, when the former Coudert Brothers law firm established a Paris office (some put this date far earlier – perhaps as early as 1879).[1] Sullivan & Cromwell was one of several New York-based firms to develop an overseas presence before World War II, in Paris first and with offices in Berlin and Buenos Aires soon after.[2] Baker & McKenzie, arguably the pioneer of the truly global firm, opened its first international office in Caracas, Venezuela in 1955.[3] By the 1970s, many prominent US-based firms had outposts in Europe, most commonly in London, Paris and Brussels. Most of London's 'Magic Circle' firms established physical presences in the United States via New York, a little later than this. By 2011 the focus was on expansion to Washington DC.[4] Firms based in other countries have also participated in this movement,[5] including early participants such as Benelux firm NautaDutilh (to New York)[6] and, more recently, China's King & Wood (to New York, Palo Alto and Tokyo)[7] and Yingke (to London).[8]

The period since the mid-1980s has seen a substantial deepening of overseas investment in law firms, mostly in response to clients themselves becoming more global. Firms that initially supported one or two overseas offices had several by the 1990s.[9] During this period these overseas offices also increased their lawyer headcount.[10]

Law firm growth tends to follow business growth geographically. In the 1990s and 2000s, the Asia-Pacific region was the site of substantial activity. Hong Kong, Japan and China each were popular destinations. The former Coudert Brothers firm claimed to have been the first foreign law firm to obtain a licence to practise in mainland China, having established a representative presence there as early as 1979, and obtained a licence when regulatory changes required, in 1992.[11] Today, China

---

1   See Carole Silver, "Globalization and the U.S. Market in Legal Services – Shifting Identities,", *Journal of Law & Policy in International Business*, 31 (2000), p 1093, 1108 (quoting Virginia Kays Veenswijk, *Coudert Brothers: A Legacy in Law: The History of America's First International Law Firm 1853–1993* (1994), p 16).

2   N Lisagor and F Lipsius, *A Law Unto Itself: The Untold Story of the Law Firm Sullivan & Cromwell* (1988).

3   Baumann, 1999

4   Linklaters opened its New York office in 1972, Allen & Overy in 1985 (H Keenlyside, *Allen & Overy The Firm 1930-1998* (1999)), Clifford Chance in 1986 (http://www.fundinguniverse.com/company-histories/ Clifford-Chance-LLP-company-History.html), and Freshfields in 1998 (http://www.pace.edu/school-of-law/about-pace-law-school/administration-0/rachel-j-littman). Slaughter and May supported an office in New York from the 1980s through 2004 (http://www.thelawyer.com/tim-clark-slaughter-and-may/125718.article). On expansion to Washington DC, see Huisman, "Top British Law Firms Navigating Washington's Waters," ALM Media (8/8/2011) (http://www.law.com/jsp/law/LawArticleFriendly.jsp?id =1202509783409&slreturn=1).

5   In fact, foreign lawyers working in New York have started a social group, (http://foreignlawyersnyc.com/ main/ page_home.html).

6   The firm opened its office in New York in 1990, (http://www.nautadutilh.com/office.xhtml? id=4&language=en).

7   King & Wood has had a New York office since 2008 (http://www.kingandwood.com/ office.aspx?id=new-york); the firm "opened a San Francisco Bay Area office in 2001" (http://www.kingandwood.com/ office.aspx?id=silicon-valley).

8   Yingke website available at http://english.yingkelawyer.com/2011/09/30/3076.html.

9   In a study of 64 international US-based law firms conducted in 2005-2006, described in Carole Silver, Nicole De Bruin Phelan and Mikaela Rabinowitz, "Between Diffusion and Distinctiveness in Globalization: U.S. Law Firms Go Glocal", *Georgetown J. Legal Ethics*, 22, p 1431 (2009), only three firms (fewer than 5%) supported just one overseas office in 2006. (The firms included in the study "are household names in the U.S. and in the global market for legal services. [They were] selected ... based on their revenues, international footprints and the availability of information on their lawyers. The firms support a total of 386 offices in 55 cities, in which slightly more than 8,700 lawyers work."), Id at p 1437 (footnotes omitted).

10   See Silver *et al*, *supra* n 9 (only 4% (16) of the 386 offices supported by the 64 firms studied supported offices staffed with a single lawyer).

11   Virginia Kays Veenswijk, *Coudert Brothers: A Legacy in Law*.

hosts nearly 200 foreign law firms. Most are in Beijing and Shanghai and include firms as diverse as Soma Tatsuo of Japan, Wenger Vieli Belser of Switzerland and Jordan's J Nassir & Partners.[12] The United Arab Emirates followed a similar pattern. Likewise, increased economic activity in Brazil has led to a growth in the number of law firms opening there, from only five in 2007 to nearly 20 in 2011.[13]

Growth has not been uniform, of course. Certain regions attract attention more slowly, sometimes despite the strong presence of commercial and financial actors. Regulatory restrictions are one reason for this. Other influences may include the ease of temporary travel and communication without an on-the-ground presence, the lack of pressure from clients to establish an in-country presence, the intensity of competition from local law firms, the availability of legal talent and onerous living conditions. Large international firms have become adept at serving clients in remote markets even without developing local offices.[14] Yet internationalisation is by no means restricted to large firms.

Although the overseas expansion of offices increased through the 1980s and 1990s, for most firms, the proportion of lawyers working in international offices compared to those in the firm's home country remained quite low. By far the majority of lawyers practised in a single jurisdiction and often did so from a head or home office. In the case of firms arising from mergers, they did so from one or two major offices.[15] Domestic activities continued to dominate, at least in terms of the number of lawyers involved in the work. According to *The American Lawyer*,[16] by as late as 1999, only approximately one-third of the top 50 global firms had more than 10% of their lawyers working outside their home countries. A decade later, in 2010, that number had increased to about half (see Figure 1 on the following page).

In 2009, exports of legal services by UK law firms totalled £3 billion (then roughly $4.75 billion) – nearly three times the total of a decade earlier.[17] In the past two decades, US trade in legal services expanded from $1,065 million (net)[18] in 1991 to $5,771 million (net) in 2010.[19] Global trade in legal services is, in itself, an economically significant business activity.

---

12   D Sawyer, "Cleary joins rush into China as Cepa II comes into force", *The Lawyer*, October 3 2005, at http://www.thelawyer.com/cleary-joins-rush-into-china-as-cepa-ii-comes-into-force/116875.article accessed on October 24 2011.

13   "Keep out: Brazilian lawyers don't want pesky foreigners poaching their clients", *The Economist*, June 23 2011, http://www.economist.com/node/18867851.

14   A variety of approaches exist, including affiliating with local law firms individually or through a law firm network (eg, Terra Lex law firm network, at http://www.terralex.org/; Lex Mundi law firm network, at http://www.lexmundi.com/), or offering service from a nearby existing office combined with regular travel (eg, Linklaters' description of its Singapore office as including lawyers serving India ("We also have members of our India team based in Singapore covering the majority of practice areas"), at http://www.linklaters.com/Locations/Pages/Singapore.aspx).

15   Jurisdictional differences also are significant on this issue. While UK firms were dominated by their London offices, in the United States it was common for firms to have substantial offices in several cities. See Silver, *supra* n. 1.

16   Michael Goldhaber, "Empire Builders," *The American Lawyer*, October 1 2011.

17   Jonathan Djanogly, justice minister, speaking at the Future of Legal Services Forum, April 14 2011, http://www.justice.gov.uk/news/features/feature140411a.htm.

18   Bureau of Economic Analysis, US International Services, Table 1, Private Services Trade by Type, 1986–1991, http://www.bea.gov/international/international_services.htm#detailedstatisticsfor.

19   Bureau of Economic Analysis, US International Services, Table 1, Trade in Services, 1999–2010, http://www.bea.gov/international/international_services.htm#detailedstatisticsfor.

Figure 1: Profitability and global reach among the world's largest law firms (the Global 50)

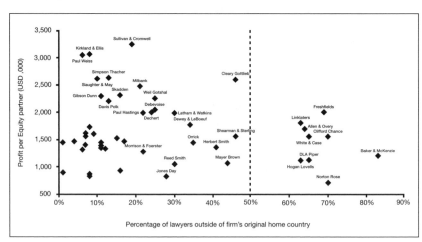

Adapted from Goldhaber, 2011

3. Drivers of international expansion in law firms

During the early period of international law firm growth, it was common for the international offices of Western firms to focus on serving clients from financially buoyant home markets that were pouring foreign direct investment (FDI) into overseas markets. This meant that the Western firms internationalised by capitalising on their existing expertise and doing in new locations what they did well at home. In this period, international and local law firms might co-exist as if on different planes of activity. As the economy shifted and businesses based in these overseas locations began to invest in more established markets, law firms redirected their efforts and broadened their attention to include serving local clients. Following the 2008 financial crisis, Western FDI in emerging markets has declined significantly, further refocusing this attention. The economic potential of Asian, Latin American and other emerging markets continues to draw investment from Western multinationals, which have receded from their moribund home markets. Deal flow has moved towards channelling emerging market FDI into Western markets and so-called south-south transactions between emerging markets (although the location of three of the four BRICs (Russia, India and China) in the Northern hemisphere makes the term a bit of a misnomer). The overseas offices of many Western firms now serve a new generation of clients from emerging markets, which in many cases are relatively new users of sophisticated international legal services.

These changes, together with the rapid closing of the gap in capabilities and sophistication between top-tier local law firms and established international firms, have brought international and local law firms into more direct competition for clients as well as for lawyers.

International law firms have traditionally claimed to have talent that is both broader in skill and of higher quality than domestic firms. Of course, this may be as much about marketing as reality. While international firms may have relationships with global clients that are unavailable to domestic firms, as well as the expertise that stems from such work, the strength and competitive advantage of local firms is often underestimated. This advantage may include longstanding relationships with clients, price advantages and their deep local knowledge of the local professional, business and regulatory regimes.

These new conditions require firms to adapt their approaches to their overseas growth in quite fundamental ways. It is not enough for a firm to rely on its home country lawyers and advice – it must invest significantly in knowledge specific to the host jurisdiction, including the business and professional culture, in order to understand and capably represent these new clients. Many firms find it highly desirable to include in their legal and/or office staff individuals who have deep knowledge and fluency in the local language, customs, norms and relationships. Even before the economic crisis, it was obvious that firms had begun to make this shift. By at least the mid-2000s, the work performed in the overseas offices of top US-based global firms was accomplished primarily by lawyers whose expertise derived from domestic education and practice experience, rather than lawyers educated and licensed in the United States.[20] The top English firms made similar staffing decisions.[21] But local variations on these approaches also exist in these cases; in China, for instance, American-born Chinese lawyers who are US-licensed and fluent Mandarin speakers are a considerable advantage for firms that practise primarily US law.[22]

Domestic firms in some of the more prominent emerging markets have also developed an international profile. Examples from China are obvious. King & Wood is perhaps the leader in this regard, with offices in Hong Kong, Tokyo, New York and Palo Alto, as well as in nine cities in China. At the time of writing, King & Wood and Australian firm Mallesons Stephen Jaques have voted to merge, reportedly as a first step in creating a new global law firm with a strong Asia-centric focus.[23] The larger Australian firms have expanded widely into Southeast Asia, while South African firms are becoming increasingly prominent in legal services elsewhere in Africa. Of course, even without an overseas presence, law firms may develop outward-looking, international perspectives. In effect, they are creating global presences at home through the combination of expertise they attract. Korean firm Kim & Chang[24] is one of several in that country to have followed this strategy.[25] It has focused on representing foreign businesses active in Korea as well as internationally focused Korean businesses.[26] To this end, these firms have developed expertise in US law as

---

20   By 2005-6, two-thirds of the 8,714 lawyers working overseas for 64 of the top US-based firms earned their legal education only in schools situated outside the United States, and 57% were licensed only in a non-US jurisdiction. See Silver *et al, supra* n 9.

21   See Sigrid Quack, "Combining National Variety: Internationalisation Strategies of European Law Firms", paper presented at conference on "Lawyers and the Construction of the Rule of Law: National and Transnational Processes" (American Bar Foundation, Chicago, March 21-22 2008.

22   See Carole Silver, "The Variable Value of US Legal Education in the Global Legal Services Market", *Georgetown Journal of Legal Ethics*, 24 (2011), p 1 (describing career paths and educational background of lawyers working in China).

23   See Joshua Freedman and James Swift, "King & Wood and Mallesons plan for post-merger globalization", *The Lawyer*, November 23 2011, http://www.thelawyer.com/king-and-wood-and-mallesons-plan-for-post-merger-globalisation/1010353.article.

well as in Korean law. Many of their Korean-educated and licensed lawyers have studied in the United States in graduate legal studies programmes. It is not unusual for these lawyers also to have passed a bar exam in the United States.

Finally, because the future shape of international growth is uncertain, our ability to predict how the business of law will be affected is clouded. Emerging markets have not uniformly and slavishly adopted Western models of jurisprudence based on liberal democratic political systems. As the world evolves into an increasingly complex, dynamic and multi-polar system, we can expect a wider range of philosophies, political systems, cultures and legal systems. This is likely to make balancing local needs within a global whole even more challenging.

4.   Regulatory constraints

Regulatory and legislative convergence is a reality in fields such as financial services and governance. This, together with the emergence of regional economic communities, World Trade Organisation initiatives to reduce trade barriers in services (including legal services) and other factors might be expected to erode trade barriers and drive a global market in legal services. But professional regulation and rights of practice continue to be remarkably local and resilient. Substantial differences still exist relating to eligibility to join the profession, legal education and rights of establishment for law firms.

In certain jurisdictions, the regulation of trade in legal services has followed a pattern of incremental liberalisation, as outlined in Figure 2. Even without liberalisation, however, law firms have been creative in adapting. For example, Baker & McKenzie describes its entry into Germany as involving protracted and contentious negotiations between the firm and the German Bar. Initially, the firm was allowed to operate only so long as it did not display its name in its offices and its German lawyers practised under their own names.[27] More significant barriers have resulted in law firms avoiding a physical presence in a jurisdiction in favour of establishing satellite practices in nearby and easily accessed cities that offer a more welcoming regulatory environment.[28]

---

24   See Kim & Chang, "About Us, Global Reach", http://www.kimchang.com/ ("The diverse expertise and multicultural backgrounds of Kim & Chang's professionals make the firm the recognized leader in providing specialized legal services for cross-border transactions. The firm's international outlook owes to the large numbers of foreign-licensed professionals who work closely with Korean professionals in each practice area and bring with them expertise in the law of their respective jurisdictions and language skills and to the education and training of Korean-licensed professionals overseas. These qualities uniquely qualify us to address the legal needs of multinational companies doing business in Korea and to advise Korean multinational companies in outbound transactions. In fact, our professionals are qualified to advise in the laws of the U.S., Japan, China, Germany, France, and the Netherlands as well as of the laws of Korea. Reflecting its global outlook, Kim & Chang pioneered the establishment of practice groups specializing in serving clients from or in Japan, China, and Europe").

25   Other firms with similar, but perhaps less extensive numbers of international lawyers, include Bae, Kim & Lee, Shin & Kim, Yoon, Yang, Kim, Shin & Yu and Lee & Ko. See Carole Silver, Jae-Hyup Lee and Jeeyoon Park, "Globalization and South Korea's Market for Legal Services: Regulatory Blockages and Collateral Circulation", working paper on file with authors.

26   See Kuk-Woon Lee, "Corporate Lawyers in Korea: An Analysis of the Big 4 Law Firms in Seoul," in *Judicial System Transformation in the Globalizing World*, ed Dai-Kwon Choi & Kahei Rokumoto (2007), p 221; Jinwon Kim, Hangukeui Lopeom [Law Firms in Korea] (2009), p 120.

27   J R Baumann, *Pioneering a global vision. The story of Baker & McKenzie* (1999).

28   The Korean-related practices of US and UK law firms have been based in Hong Kong for some time prior to Korea's liberalisation of its regulation of legal services. See, for example, Paul Hastings, professional biography of Jong Han Kim, http://www.paulhastings.com/professionalDetail.aspx?ProfessionalId =12294.

Figure 2: The progression of liberalisation of legal services followed in some markets

Closed market	International practices	Limited full practice	Unrestricted practice
Foreign law firms are prohibited from practising law from a local base, although alliances with local firms are usually allowed.	Foreign law firms are permitted to establish a local presence in order to practise international law only, but are prohibited from employing locally qualified lawyers, so rendering the practice of local law illegal.	Foreign law firms are permitted to establish a local presence and a specified proportion of locally qualified lawyers is allowed, so the practice of local law is permissible.	Foreign law firms have no more restrictions placed upon them than those that apply also to local law firms.
India		A prescribed percentage of the equity in the firm may also be required to be locally owned.	United States United Kingdom European Union Canada Australia
	Alliances with local firms are permitted and often encouraged		
	Brazil Indonesia China	Singapore	

Liberalisation can be built into a jurisdiction's regulatory structure. Korea provides a nice example. Until recently, foreign law firms in Korea have not been allowed to establish local presences. Following the country's free trade agreements with the European Union and United States, however, regulatory barriers will be loosened in three stages over the next few years. In the first stage, EU and US lawyers and law firms will be able to establish branch offices from which they may offer advice on foreign and international law. The second stage, which will begin within two years of the effective date of the agreements, will permit EU and US firms to share fees with Korean law firms, on either a single-project or ongoing basis. Finally, under the third and final stage, to begin within five years, Korean lawyers may enter into partnerships with EU and US lawyers; in addition, EU and US firms will be allowed to employ Korean lawyers.

In other jurisdictions, the direction of liberalisation is more complex. In the United States, for example, every state determines its own rules governing the legal profession. Consequently, liberalisation in the United States is not uniform. Moreover, and apart from the United States, while every jurisdiction has not taken a path towards liberalisation, so too revisions to regulatory regimes are not necessarily equivalent to liberalisation. In England and Wales, for example, where the legal services sector is currently in the throes of quite transformational change, the newly constituted Solicitors Regulatory Authority tends to use the term 're-regulation', rather than de-regulation, to emphasise that the regulatory framework is changing rather than being discarded.[29] In some respects, international firms may find it harder to overcome tensions between global and local priorities in re-regulated markets, particularly with regard to such radically different features as non-lawyer equity ownership and multidisciplinary practices. On the other hand, several non-UK providers of legal services may consider establishing legal services businesses in the United Kingdom precisely because of the flexibility provided by the Legal Services Act.[30]

5.   Strategies for internationalisation

Many considerations shape the decision to pursue a strategy of international growth. They also shape how to effect entry into a new market. Some of the most common include:

- the views of the firm's most important clients that would be affected by such a move;
- the nature of the firm's intended practice in a particular location (eg, its substantive focus) and whether it intends to advise on local law;
- the level of investment that the firm can afford to make, which may relate to the number of lawyers supported in a location, among other things;
- the local regulatory environment governing the practice of law, including the degree of clarity or ambiguity in the governing rules;
- the intensity of competition, whether from local or international law firms or other organisations;
- socio-political, economic and other risk factors;
- the ability to attract and retain key talent in the location;
- the availability of a suitable merger or alliance partner, or of trusted local referral firms with which to establish referral or 'best friend' relationships; and
- the firm's ability to offer competitive prices to its target clients.

These factors may not be independent of one another, rendering a one-size-fits-all approach untenable. Nevertheless, in many instances balancing the level of investment required to establish a platform that clients will find attractive with the long-term economic potential is probably the most compelling consideration.

In this context, a range of options are available to a firm that is planning to enter

---

29   See Jayne Willetts, "Management and Reporting Obligations under the New Handbook", Regulation Report, www.birminghamlawsociety.co.uk ("At this stage of the process it is interesting to note the changes that have been highlighted by the SRA in this latest phase of this fundamental re-regulation project. There had been widespread claims that outcomes-focused regulation ('OFR') would represent a significant reduction in the degree of regulation that law firms would be subject to, but the SRA now seem to be going to some lengths to deny that this is the case").

30   "Top City lawyer targets Chinese and Indian law firms for ABS launch", *Legal Futures* August 11 2011, http://www.legalfutures.co.uk/legal-services-act/market-monitor/top-city-lawyer-targets-chinese-and-indian-law-firms-for-abs-launch.

a particular jurisdiction or expand within it. These are outlined in Figure 3 and discussed in more detail below.

Figure 3: A continuum of possible levels of involvement in a local market, from no formal links to a full local office practising both international and local law

---

1. No formal links

No local presence or formal bilateral links with legal service providers in the market. Links solely through the International Bar Association or through affiliation with a global law firm network such as Lex Mundi.

2. Best friend

No local presence, but usually an informal, bilateral referral agreeement (at least) with a local firm, usually transactional in nature, but may also extend to limited knowledge-sharing secondments etc in order to enhance the relationship.

3. Remote alliance

No local presence, but a formal bilateral referral agreeement with a local firm usually extends beyond the transactional to include joint business development and other collaboration, both to enhance relationships and to deepen the capabilities of the local firm.

4. Local alliance

The international firm has a local presence, practising only foreign law. Local law is delivered through a formal alliance with a local firm. The alliance includes a range of collaboration initiatives to grow each others' business, enhance relationships and deepen capabilities.

5. Full local office

The international firm has a local presence that practises both foreign and local law, in essence similarly to indigenous firms, through not necessarily delivering the full range of local services.

5.1   No formal links

In many instances, the relationship of a law firm to a particular jurisdiction is neither sufficiently ongoing nor recurring to warrant special investment. Under such circumstances, firms may rely simply on referral relationships with local lawyers and law firms that provide expertise on local law. The difficulties of such occasional relationships typically involve issues of quality and risks of availability, expertise and price. To minimise these uncertainties, firms may use a variety of mechanisms to become acquainted with local lawyers, law firms and professional norms, including law firm networks, professional association activities and other opportunities.

A variation on this model is when firms develop dedicated teams that are focused on particular jurisdictions but located in an office (or offices) outside the target jurisdiction. In some cases – such as India and, until 2011, Korea – regulatory constraints demand such an approach. Many US firms with interests in Latin America use this approach for that region, some maintaining quite large Latin American teams in their US offices. Some firms continue to use country or regional 'desks' to coordinate their activities in a market or region in which they do not have an actual presence.

5.2 Best friends

In markets in which law firms have frequent interaction, repeated referrals may morph into one or more 'best-friend' relationships. The term is most strongly associated with the UK law firm Slaughter and May, whose strategy has been to limit its number of offices (currently a main office in London and branches in Brussels, Hong Kong and Beijing) and instead work "with law firms that are leaders in their jurisdictions ... to provide clients with a 'best of the best' global legal service".[31] Best-friend relationships, in this sense, may involve more than mere referrals. Firms may also build relationships among their lawyers in order to develop common knowledge and approaches. In order to cement the relationships, firms may second lawyers between them, share knowledge and make joint pitches to clients. Relationships may be non-exclusive or (more rarely) exclusive. Multi-jurisdictional networks of law firms, such as Lex Mundi and Terralex, are also organised along these lines. Successful strategies for maintaining 'best-friend' relationships include active management, frequent contact between lawyers of different firms and steps from each firm to cement and broaden their ties.

In markets with very restrictive regulatory environments, a best-friend relationship may be the closest relationship that is possible.

5.3 Alliances

An alliance takes the notion of 'best friend' closer to permanence and formality. Alliances give structure to a relationship, often by explicitly identifying terms and strategic objectives through a formal agreement. These may include jointly winning market share in a particular region, jointly serving a number of clients or supporting one another in substantive areas of practice. Alliances among law firms are frequently non-exclusive. Successful alliances often have joint governance structures and clearly defined measures of success. It is important for firms to monitor and discuss progress towards joint strategic objectives on a regular basis. Clarity is critical to maintaining alliances, particularly in defining the scope and intent of the alliance. Mismatched expectations – especially with regard to the level of input that each party may expect of the other, and whether the alliance will eventually transform into a closer relationship – are common hazards.

Alliances may be local or remote. Remote alliances exist when an international law firm does not have a physical presence in the local market, but relies on the local ally as its proxy. A local alliance, by contrast, involves collaboration between the offices of the international and local firms in the same location. At an extreme, the offices of local alliance firms actually may be next to each other and even share some

---

31   Slaughter and May website, at http://www.slaughterandmay.com/where-we-work/global-reach.aspx.

services. This arrangement is common in markets where an international firm is prevented by regulation from advising on local law, but local law advice is vital to its work; or where regulatory change is expected and firms position themselves to combine whenever possible.

5.4 Local office

A local office usually represents a deep investment in a market. Traditionally, local offices of law firms have tended to emulate the pyramid structure of the larger or head offices. But advances in technology and the need that some see for wider global coverage are driving firms to adopt more diverse structural models. Deciding to support a local office does not determine the staffing of that office. Rather, staffing decisions relate to the expertise required, the available talent and any local regulatory constraints. Firms may use local offices to advise solely on international or foreign law, or also develop expertise in local law. Similarly, firms may specialise in particular substantive areas, such as international litigation and arbitration, intellectual property or mergers and acquisitions, or may take a more generalist approach.[32]

Various mechanisms also exist for developing a local office. These include acquiring an existing local law firm, cherry-picking groups of lawyers from local firms or developing an office through a greenfield investment. The greenfield approach can begin quite modestly. It may even be funded by a large client matter in the jurisdiction. An office may comprise no more than a single lawyer, who may be a national of the host country and authorised to practise locally. Such a cautious approach keeps initial investments to a minimum and may encourage the new office to fund its own growth.

Each of these options brings its own challenges. For example, it may be that a willing acquisition or merger candidate exists, but the aspirations of the local firm do not align well with the overarching global strategy of the international firm. Firms often underestimate the amount of effort and cost involved in reshaping an acquired office to fit a global whole, especially if significant severance costs are incurred as the business moves from an independent firm to affiliation with a large international firm. The human costs of such restructuring – damage to morale, collegiality and levels of trust – can be as significant as the financial. On the other hand, acquiring a local firm delivers ready-made relationships, infrastructure and, sometimes, cash flow. Decisions on these matters may remain fluid as firms become more comfortable in particular jurisdictions and economic and regulatory influences change.

6. Aligning local and global strategies

Developing an international strategy is not simply about determining which approach to growth is most appropriate for a particular firm at a particular time. It also means considering the consequences of such decisions. These consequences involve at least three layers of analysis:

- First, how does the market for legal services in the target jurisdiction differ

---

32   See Silver *et al*, *supra* n 9 (describing substantive areas of practice of overseas offices).

from the firm's home market?[33]

- Second, what are the implications of these differences? What tensions are likely to arise between the needs induced by the particular market characteristics of the target jurisdiction and the firm's overall strategy, structure and objectives?
- Third, how will efforts to balance these tensions influence the firm's ability to service its clients in ways that sustain long-term client relationships and enable it to deliver competitive economic performance?

Law and lawyer regulation can be considered additional frames of complexity. However, law firms must also address the wider social, economic, political and cultural issues that challenge the efforts of multinational corporations to align local business units within a congruent global whole, while sustaining and improving their economic performance and long-term competitive advantage. These may be the most significant challenges to balancing local and global priorities.

6.1 Managing tensions between local and global strategies

As firms consider whether and how to enter a particular jurisdiction and embrace an international strategy, they face many decisions that demand the management of local and global needs. In some cases, the sequence of events that leads to an initial investment in a particular location may become outdated as new regulatory regimes are adopted or the economic climate changes. How a firm enters the market, particularly if through a merger or acquisition of a local law firm, may require that local entity to be reshaped so as to conform with the firm's global strategy. There may be duplications and redundancies of staff, and certain areas of the local firm's practice may create conflicts or simply be incompatible with the overall strategy. Local offices may evolve into different structures, tied to their new firms by new organisational arrangements.

When addressing these tensions, firms may be influenced by a number of issues. These are described in the following sections.

(a) How much autonomy is delegated to the local office

Some functions, such as managing conflicts and setting the overall strategic direction, must be steered centrally. Marketing and human resource management may, at least partially, be best managed locally or regionally. Many functions of the firm will benefit from a carefully managed interaction between global, regional and local levels. Guidelines can be set at the global level so as to protect and advance the firm's brand and ensure consistent standards, but beyond this firms may wish to defer to local conditions and approaches.

---

33 In the context of law firms, differences may manifest themselves in three distinct ways:
- differences in the substantive law, including underlying concepts of jurisprudence and judicial processes;
- differences in the practice of law, including the unique attributes of the legal profession in a particular jurisdiction; and
- differences in social and cultural norms and ways of doing business.

If too much authority is delegated to local offices, local partners may develop views of the firm's strategy and systems that are at variance with those of the whole. This may lead to inefficiencies, brand dilution, service inconsistences and, worst of all, damaged relationships with key clients. Too little authority, if the centre is not well attuned to the needs of local markets, may also harm performance. Decision-making processes may be less than agile. Transplanting action taken in one jurisdiction to another may also be inappropriate and ineffective – that is, one size does not fit all.

(b) **Whether local law is to be practised**
In many cases, an international firm entering a new market will require access to local lawyers. Having those lawyers practise within the firm reduces risk by keeping them within the firm's systems and structures. On the other hand, if the firm's intent in the jurisdiction is primarily to serve international clients in matters of foreign or international law, it may be difficult to keep the local lawyers sufficiently busy with work that is consistent with the firm's strategy. Expanding the spectrum of work that these lawyers do, to include services inconsistent with the firm's core offerings, may dilute the firm's brand. In some emerging economies, intense competition with existing local firms may also make it difficult to achieve the fee levels needed to justify a local presence.

(c) **Quality control**
Ensuring a consistent level of quality, both substantively and in terms of managing client and other relationships, across offices and jurisdictions is one of the most serious challenges facing multi-jurisdictional law firms. Managing this means, among other things:
- developing robust knowledge and learning processes, and sharing them between offices;
- frequently moving lawyers between offices, whether on individual matters, short-term secondments or even longer-term assignments; and
- proactively encouraging the development of practice, sector and/or client teams across offices.

(d) **Availability of management time and other resources**
Establishing new offices can be expensive and time consuming. Resources spent on the new office must be diverted from other pressing issues. Firms in which offices act more like equal peers than under a top-down management structure, and that are characterised by significant delegation of management discretion, may be more likely to establish multiple overseas offices. However, they may also develop redundant and inefficient structures and systems.

(e) **Varying levels of contribution to profitability**
One of the most substantial tensions for firms with multiple international offices is the variable contribution to profits made by different offices and the consequent variations in partner and lawyer compensation. An excessive preoccupation with identifying offices that increase or decrease profitability can be damaging,

particularly to lawyers in offices located in jurisdictions where the market itself is weaker or whose practice is in a cyclical downturn. By definition, 50% of all revenues in any firm in which office contribution is not uniform are dilutive, and the other 50% accretive. The issue of relative contributions may be more or less problematic depending on a firm's compensation system. Firms with performance-based partner compensation systems, for example, may consider such differences less compelling than firms with lockstep systems, because (in theory at least) compensation with self-correct for performance or contributions to profitability. Location also matters. It is easier to manage this in firms in which most lawyers work in economically similar jurisdictions, so that the number of partners requiring subsidisation is small.

(f)   Varying net partner income

Personal income tax, cost of living and other issues not directly related to practising law in a particular jurisdiction also create financial disparities between partners. This is one reason why lawyers may prefer to practise in particular jurisdictions, such as Hong Kong and Singapore, that impose relatively low tax rates. For partners in UK law firms, for example, who in 2011 already pay a 50% marginal rate of personal income tax, the idea of subsidising partners in other high-tax jurisdictions is anathema. Efforts to establish and develop offices in high-tax jurisdictions, consequently, can be starved for lack of experienced talent. The ease with which US law firms have been able to attract experienced partners away from UK firms in China is at least partly due to their greater appetite to invest in higher compensation for their China-based partners.

(g)   Organisational structure

Multinational law firms are complex social organisations. They exist to a large degree because of the potential for referring work across jurisdictions and among offices. Work is frequently performed in offices other than that in which a matter originated. It may even be allocated across multiple offices. How, then, does one encourage sharing of clients and work while optimising economic performance and sustainable competitive advantage across diverse jurisdictions? The solution used by the 'Big 4' accounting firms,[34] Baker & McKenzie and others involves a particular organisational form – the Swiss *Verein*. *Vereins* accommodate a variety of business entities situated in different jurisdictions.[35] Besides Baker & McKenzie, other firms to have adopted this structure include DLA Piper, Hogan Lovells, Norton Rose and SNR Denton. Its

---

34   The Big 4 accounting firms have subsequently changed their holding structures from Swiss *Vereins* to private companies limited by guarantee, registered in London, largely in order to manage inter-jurisdictional transfers of risk. Opinions vary the degree to which global law firms should follow suit.

35   On *Vereins* generally, see Megan Vetula, Note, "From The Big Four to Big Law: The Swiss Verein and The Global Law Firm", 22 *Georgetown Journal of Legal Ethics*, 22 (2009), p 1177.

36   See Matt Byrne, "*Vereins*: To *verein* or not *verein*", The Lawyer, August 15 2011) http://www.thelawyer.com/the-lawyer-uk-200-preview-vereins-to-verein-or-not-verein/1008940.article ("Under these vehicles, the component firms make contributions to cover central costs but do not share profits. Purists argue these are not real mergers. They claim the lack of financial integration suggests they are nothing more than glorified associations along the lines of Lex Mundi. Often those jurisdictions have lower profitability levels, adding grist to rivals' mill that the main reason for not integrating is to avoid diluting profits"); Peter Kalis, "Grand Illusion", *The American Lawyer*, May 2011.

primary advantage is flexibility – it allows different strategies for different markets and even separate profit pools. In addition, *Vereins* are not difficult or expensive to establish. Some say that a *Verein* does not constitute a proper merger, arguing that the coalition of offices within this structure is not coherent enough to be considered a single firm.[36] But if this is true, then the assertion must be applied as much to the 'Big 4' accounting firms as to the law firms. There is also some debate regarding its effectiveness for limiting trans-jurisdictional risk, although this usually is not the primary reason that global law firms adopt the structure.

Firms use the *Verein* in different ways to enhance partner performance and define compensation. Common factors influencing these decisions include the number of partnership tiers and the relationships between them, the design of the partner compensation system and the accounting principles used in the firm (and whether all offices are on the same system).

7.   Conclusion

Just as there is no universal approach to managing the challenges of globalisation, the issues raised by global strategies also vary. Still, we have tried in this chapter to suggest several basic considerations. Jurisdictional differences are often more significant than initially anticipated, and regulation sometimes represents only a small part of these. Strategies that place too much emphasis on international standardisation and on increasing scale for its own sake can be dangerous under these circumstances. While firms may take advantage of similarities across borders, it is perhaps more important that they recognise and embrace local variations. Firms that acknowledge jurisdictional differences rather than treating them as inconsistencies to be overcome are likely to find greater success, both in satisfying client needs and in creating hospitable environments for their lawyers.

Profitability drivers and financing techniques for law firms

James Tsolakis
The Royal Bank of Scotland

The business of law is not only concerned with receiving and executing legal instructions. It also involves disciplines in conducting the business of the law firm itself. Executing these disciplines according to prudent business and financial principles will give the firm financial stability, and fee earners will thereby be permitted to focus on their client relationships.

1. Cash-flow management

The financial success of a law firm depends very much on its ability to generate cash. This requires active management of the working capital requirements of the firm and the cash-flow cycle. This cycle will vary between firms, depending on the nature of the work, the type of client base, the firm's geography, local customs and practices, the resources that the firm commits in terms of both fee earners and back-office staff, and the technology that is available.

Cash generated by a law firm is a function of fee income. It results from the processes of billing and collection. Active management of work-in-progress (WIP) and debtors' lock-up is therefore critical. Most firms will set targets for the number of days of fees outstanding in WIP and debtors. Increasingly, these targets are being handed down to practice groups and, in turn, to individual partners. As an extension of this practice, partners are often held personally accountable for billing and collection targets. Not meeting these targets may directly affect partner compensation and the amount and timing of that partner's distributions from the firm.

Regular billing and collection are therefore critical features of good cash-flow management. As already indicated, however, the characteristics of different practice areas will drive billing and collection cycles. Instructions in practice areas such as personal injury and contingent fee litigation, for example, will typically take longer to conclude than, say, a typical corporate or banking practice instruction. Personal injury practices will therefore be expected to have longer billing and collection cycles than other practices. In addition, billings and collections typically show a seasonal pattern. There is often a heavy emphasis on billing before year end for firms that are following the accrual accounting convention, and a very heavy emphasis on cash collections prior to year end for firms following the cash accounting convention. This maximises the revenue recognition for these firms, and in the latter case also the cash available for distribution to partners.

To mitigate the adverse impact on cash flow of lengthy instructions, many firms have introduced interim billing arrangements. These generate some cash, although usually not the full value of the work undertaken. Contingent fee arrangements can be managed in the same way.

Controlling credit around the firm's client base is critical to its success. Credit can be controlled by maximising the value of debtor recovery or minimising the number of debtors written off as bad debts. This process begins with the running of appropriate credit checks on new clients admitted to the firm and extends to periodic reviews of the credit quality of the firm's client base. Finally, as firms have expanded they have benefited from a team that is accountable for the collection of outstanding debtors, and is independent of partners and other fee earners.

There are risks if the client base is too concentrated. Excessive exposure to a single client could leave the firm at serious risk of loss if that client's credit quality deteriorates or the client fails. Most firms set limits on their financial exposure to any client and the maximum amount that any single client can represent of the firm's total fees.

One cannot underestimate the importance of good technology in managing WIP, debtors and collections. Many firms have underinvested in this area, and this has proven to be detrimental to generating cash flow and improving the cash flow cycle. More forward-thinking firms have taken a long-term view of the importance of investing in technology. After several years, they are now reaping the rewards of a superior technology platform.

Turning to the question of cash outgoings, several factors can help to improve the cash-flow cycle. These recognise the opportunity to proactively manage cash outgoings. They include:

- staff salaries (flexible hours dependent on availability of billable work);
- rents (deferrals depending on lease terms); and
- partner distributions, which are usually non-contractual and paid at the discretion of management.

Some UK firms also derive significant benefits in cash flow and working capital by retaining partner earnings in advance of paying their tax remittances in January and July in each year. Accumulated cash balances that are earmarked to pay partners' taxes may be used as an additional source of working capital on top of any overdraft and revolving credit facilities provided by the bank.

Finally, it should be remembered that profitability is a poor proxy for cash-flow. Firms may be exceptionally profitable, but those that do not recognise the critical importance of converting profits into cash may struggle to survive.

2.   Funding

Historically, the financing techniques applied by the legal profession have been narrowly based. Although they still dominate firms' funding structures, these traditional techniques are now expanding to include financing alternatives that are more commonly in place in the larger corporate and institutional borrowing markets. While an increasingly wide variety of funding sources is available to the legal profession, these will not be available to firms of smaller sizes. Nor will they be available in all jurisdictions. However, the markets are rapidly evolving, and it is likely that current developments in more advanced markets will be adopted more widely by more firms and across more geographies.

2.1 Bank overdrafts

Bank overdrafts are typically on-demand credit facilities that provide firms access to same-day funding. They are usually priced at a margin over the official central bank benchmark rate (in the United Kingdom this is the Bank of England's base rate). The purpose of bank overdrafts is to handle intra and end-of-day cash-flow shortfalls between a firm's collections and payments. If bank overdrafts are outstanding for a prolonged period, this may suggest that the firm has some broader problems of cash flow and cash collection. It may also be a symptom of a firm overtrading, a poorly structured capital structure that needs debt facilities with a longer maturity profile or insufficient partner capital.

2.2 Revolving credit facilities

Revolving credit facilities are usually committed lines of credit. They usually have a maturity of three years, but this may be as much as five. They are usually priced at a margin over the London Interbank Offered Rate (LIBOR) or the equivalent benchmark rate in the relevant jurisdiction. Revolving credit facilities are intended to provide firms with the certainty of financing working capital. This is particularly visible during periods of growth when WIP and debtors require financing, and also during the seasonal fluctuations when collections slow down or large and irregular payments are required (eg, tax obligations).

2.3 Short-term loans

Banks and specialist finance houses with dedicated teams focused on the legal sector have developed loan products to service certain seasonal and recurring outgoings in the legal profession. These loans are particularly designed to finance annual professional indemnity insurance premiums, semi-annual taxation payments and annual practising certificate costs. They generally have a maturity of 10 to 12 months, are usually fixed rate and are paid off fully in equal monthly instalments over the life of the loan. The loans spread the costs of large and typically annual expenses over a period that is more like the period over which the benefits of these expenses accrue. In addition, because the loans are usually fixed rate, their cash cost can be precisely quantified, thereby helping the firm to plan, budget and forecast cash flow more accurately.

2.4 Equipment finance

Finance for office equipment is normally provided in the form of term debt with a maturity profile similar to the useful life of the underlying asset. In recent years, as the cost of bank equity capital and debt capital has risen, so has the cost of providing longer-term finance. As a result, finance for purchasing equipment has tended to mature in five years or less. Other forms of finance can be used for buying office equipment. These include both leasing and hire purchase agreements. In both cases, specialist finance houses have begun to offer a range of products designed to meet the needs of the legal profession. In almost all cases, the financing is provided on an amortising basis over the life of the loan, often with a residual or balloon payment at maturity.

2.5   Term loans

Law firms primarily use term loans to pay for office moves or new premises. These loans are normally long term, with a maturity profile that matches the underlying asset that they are financing. In recent years, the maturity profile of loans for this purpose has shortened and loans with a five-year maturity are now readily available. Longer maturities are also possible, but they are much harder to find. As with revolving credit facilities, term loans are usually priced at a margin over the LIBOR or the equivalent benchmark rate. In some cases they may be structured with a revolving credit facility and an overdraft, so as to provide the borrower with multi-functional credit arrangements in one loan agreement. In my experience, approximately 30% to 40% of the costs of an office move are in durable, identifiable and moveable assets that can be financed through one of the specialist houses that finances office equipment. This leaves 60% to 70% of the capital cost of the new premises to be financed in the bank market. A positive feature of the commercial real estate market in the United Kingdom at the moment is that the oversupply of new untenanted premises has led property developers and landlords to offer some attractive deals. Tenants may now be offered up to three years' rent so as to fit out new premises or be invited to occupy the building rent free for a similar period.

2.6   Creditors and suppliers

A law firm's creditors and suppliers will usually extend credit to their customers. While this is not direct funding, the effect of the trade terms available represent an extension of credit during which time the firm is not required to pay for the products or services delivered. A firm's purchases that are subject to these arrangements are usually modest. However, if the firm is an important customer of the supplier, extended credit terms may be available. If these can be negotiated, a modest but positive impact on cash flow is available.

2.7   Partners

Partners fund their law firms directly via the injection of capital and through profit retentions. This is discussed in more detail below.

3.   Capital financing

The methods by which law firms are capitalised have been standard and predictable for a long time. However, they are now evolving and significant new models can be expected to emerge in the near future.

3.1   Partners

The initial financial responsibility and burden rests with the partners, as a firm's owners. Partners may use their savings to provide the initial capital required to support entry into the practice of law, and also the additional capital requirements of a firm to support its growth over time.

3.2 Partner borrowings

As an alternative to using their savings, some partners may choose to borrow some or all of the necessary funds from a bank. Banks familiar with the legal sector often have dedicated teams to support the needs of the legal profession, and have proven, standardised processes and documentation for providing partners with capital loans. This type of financing can be very tax effective for individuals. In the United Kingdom, for example, in most cases the interest payable on the loans is an allowable deduction.

3.3 Profit retention

Many firms have introduced capital retention programmes as a way of building capital. These programmes hold back a percentage of partner distributions during the year and accumulate them in the partner's capital accounts. This is a very useful way of gradually increasing a firm's capital. When a firm is growing organically, through the lateral hiring of partners or through larger acquisitions, its capital structure may be strained. The effect of this can be mitigated by partners reinvesting in the business throughout the year and so building the firm's capital base. In larger firms in particular, there is a trend to retain profits to provide for future long-term financial stability. In this way, capital growth is given priority over larger short-term distributions and income returns. The uncertain global economic conditions at present and the greater competitive pressures of the legal market make this a prudent approach to financial management. It is likely to position firms better for the business and financial challenges that they will face in the future.

3.4 Corporate loans

As an alternative to partners borrowing directly, structures have emerged in which the borrowing is undertaken by the firm or a finance vehicle owned by the firm, and guaranteed or supported with some direct recourse to the partners. For larger firms, this simplifies the significant administrative burden that is associated with a large number of individual partner capital loans by replacing them with a single loan. Corporate loans may also be available at a lower cost than individual partner capital loans. They also ensure that all partners are financing the firm on the same terms. However, partners with the available liquidity may be prevented from investing directly in the firm and may be forced to bear a share of the interest burden of a corporate loan arrangement.

3.5 Equity capital markets

Historically, the equity capital markets have not been an available source of capital for law firms. Following deregulation of the marketplace in Australia, Slater and Gordon successfully completed an initial public offering in May 2007. It was able to raise equity capital of A$35 million in the public markets.

This is the only example of a law firm business listed and traded on a stock exchange, but it establishes a precedent that other firms can be expected to follow as their regulatory environments allow it. This change is already occurring in the United Kingdom with the effect of the Legal Services Act (2007), which will go into force under the supervision of the Legal Services Board. This reform allows UK law firms to access third-party capital. It has been reported[1] that Irwin Mitchell will complete an initial public offering once these rules are in place. However, a rush of activity in this area is not expected. The business plans of most firms are not constrained by a lack of capital. If, however, a firm is planning rapid expansion, to become a consolidator in an overpopulated and fragmented market, then equity capital markets may provide an attractive source of finance. The trade-off is a dilution of the existing equity, a loss of control, more corporate governance, public visibility and accountability, and a more costly operating environment.

3.6 Private equity

Following the deregulation of the market for legal services in the United Kingdom, private equity firms will be able to buy into law firms. There is no doubt that significant amounts of money are being held in private equity for this purpose. Private equity firms are frustrated by the lack of investment opportunities that meet their criteria. In particular, there do not seem to be many opportunities to create the required target returns, and the exit strategy and timing are ill-defined. However, a portion of the capital of UK firm QualitySolicitors was recently reported[2] to have been sold to private equity firm Palamon Capital Partners, with the proceeds used for marketing and operational purposes supporting the firm's goal to achieve growth in the retail sector of the legal market.

3.7 Alternative business structures

In the United Kingdom, the Legal Services Act allows for changes in the ownership structure and control of the legal profession. It permits the formation of legal disciplinary practices, involving a combination of legal practitioners across different legal disciplines – for example, solicitors and barristers – with up to 25% non-lawyer partners. The act also allows legal disciplinary practices to transfer to multi-disciplinary practices in which law can be practised within the legal and organisational structure of another business, such as a retailer, bank, insurance company, accountant or surveyor. The capital available from these other business should provide for the increasing capital needs of the more broadly based law firm.

4. Profitability dynamics

The profitability dynamics of a law firm are a function of a number of factors. Some of these are within the firm's control, while others are a function of the economic, legal and regulatory environment in which it operates.

Some of the controllable factors are financial and others are not. Non-financial factors include:

- the firm's location;
- whether it is single or multiple office;
- whether its operations are local, national, regional, international or global in scope;

---

1   *The Lawyer*, April 25 2011
2   *Legal Week*, October 20 2011

- its best-friend arrangements;
- its practice areas;
- whether it is generalist or specialist;
- its criteria for choosing clients; and
- the qualifications of its lawyers and partners.

Once strategic choices have been made about each of these factors, they will drive the type of instructions that the firm receives, the clients that provide them and where they are executed. In turn, this will drive some of the financial criteria that determine the firm's profitability.

There are many ways to measure the success of a law firm. However, in terms of financial success the profits available to the owners or equity partners is the most common measure. Put simply, firms must maximise revenues and minimise costs.

Revenues are a product of the billable hours worked by fee earners and the billing rate at which they are charged. Fee earners in most financially successful law firms work more than the average number of hours and the rate charged is above average. Certain personal and lifestyle choices are therefore essential to superior financial success. Premium fees are still a feature of the market for the right instructions, although they are less common than they were before the credit crisis of 2008. Another characteristic of most financially successful firms is a below-average write-down of WIP for billing purposes. Firms that can consistently obtain a full or high recovery of WIP tend to outperform their peers. In an environment in which billing rates continue to be under pressure from general counsel keen to strike more attractive deals, and clients looking more generally for savings in legal fees and cheaper legal services, the outlook for driving financial success through high recoveries and resilient fee income growth is challenging.

High lawyer leverage is another way to improve profitability. It is not in itself the key to success, however. In many firms that offer clients high-value, bespoke advice, the lawyer leverage is low, at below 2:1. On the other hand, firms that are instructed on large multi-part, multi-dimensional and sometimes cross-jurisdictional transactions will have a high lawyer leverage, at above 5:1. These firms may also deliver above-average partner earnings. Finally, some firms with high-volume and low-value instructions that entail highly replicable legal processes (eg, residential mortgage, personal injury) are likely to have lawyer leverage well above 5:1.

Lawyer leverage is just one of the tools available to management to improve the firm's financial outcomes. Ultimately, however, it is driven by the firm's strategic choices about the law to be practised and the clients to work for. This will in turn define the complexity of client instructions received and the best business model and lawyer leverage to complete them. In the final analysis, clients will determine how well the model works by the immediate feedback they give on transaction success and their willingness to offer follow-up instructions.

Expense management is critical to profitability. It has been a high priority for most law firms during the economic downturn. Firms must continue to be rigorous in managing their expenses in a global economy that is still uncertain and a market characterised by little growth, continuing price pressure and low volumes of transactions. Law firms need to be consistent in controlling expenses so as to eliminate unnecessary costs, deliver material savings and create leaner, more efficient and nimble organisations.

It is important to recognise that the non-salary and wage components make up a relatively small part of a firm's total costs. Therefore, the relative gains become smaller as the opportunities for further cost cutting decrease.

The current trend is to outsource back office and fee earner functions, with the aim of creating a more competitive cost base and business model. We expect this to continue. Momentum is building behind the trend as it makes material savings available and gives firms an advantage over their competitors. As an extension of this, firms are increasingly challenging their business models and traditional practices:

- The location in which they choose to execute client instructions may be moved out of the main office to a cheaper location.
- Technology is being employed to process and speed up functions that can be automated.
- Paralegals and non-qualified staff are being employed to execute those parts of client instructions and transactions that do not require a fully qualified lawyer.

As firms become more international in scope, we expect the effect of foreign exchange volatility to have a greater impact on those activities. In some instances, especially in 2009, many firms made more than 10% of their revenues thanks to favourable foreign exchange movements. With greater global economic uncertainty, and more volatile foreign exchanges, we expect firms to place more emphasis on mitigating the potential risk of foreign exchange losses.

Responsibility for the financial management of a law firm rests clearly with its leadership team and management. Over the last decade there has been a material change in the resources firms commit to financial management. This change can be seen in both the experience of individuals occupying the senior financial roles and the resources that are committed to the finance function.

Historically, the finance function was a by-product of the financial accounting and reporting activities. Today, however, senior career professionals in finance roles are increasingly being introduced from non-legal and more general corporate backgrounds. This brings new perspectives and an independent view of how to introduce or implement corporate best practices in treasury and financial management as they apply in a legal environment.

Whether a firm can improve its finance function will be driven by its financial strength and resources. Smaller firms will naturally be less able to commit significant resources to this. However, this does not mean that it is any less important in a smaller environment. Outsourcing solutions, through either dedicated companies or local accountancy firms, may be an attractive alternative.

Regardless of the size of the firm, strong financial management needs to come from the top. It is the responsibility of management to set the parameters for acceptable performance and standards of excellence. The firm's financial management must be aligned with these so that all of the relevant criteria can be measured and reported in a timely fashion and appropriate action taken to ensure satisfactory financial performance.

5. Business and financial disciplines

The favourable business conditions before 2008 insulated the legal profession from the need for the financial rigour and discipline of the wider business community. Yet recently, the profession has begun to take these principles on as energetically as other areas of the business community. This has been the case particularly for the larger and more global firms.

Firms are being forced to adapt in response to the still-challenging economic conditions, increased domestic and international competition, deregulation of the legal profession in some markets and a client base that is increasingly demanding better service and attention for more favourable fees.

Corporate governance issues are becoming ever more important. Firms are becoming more transparent about their activities, not only with their partners, but also with other stakeholders such as staff, clients, regulators, the community, banks and suppliers.

As this process develops, some of the areas requiring a new or renewed focus include:

- a clearly defined strategy setting out the firm's vision and goals for the future;
- a detailed business plan describing how the business and financial goals of the firm as defined by the strategy will be accomplished;
- financial plans and budgets in support of the business activities, initiatives and investments described in the business plan;
- regular, timely, accurate and reliable financial information so as to assess performance against the plan. A detailed analysis of material deviations from plan, whether favourable or unfavourable, is required; and
- a process for sharing results and performance with partners and staff, so that responsible individuals can be held accountable for their performance and have it acknowledged against the firm's plans.

These are not areas in which law firms – even the very successful ones – have excelled in the past. However, firms are improving their skills dramatically and the culture of firms is changing quickly as these principles become more embedded into firms' core values and cultures.

Building a business: winning clients and adding value to the practice

Norman Clark
Walker Clark, LLC

1, Introduction

Building a successful legal practice is more difficult today than ever before. In most jurisdictions, the competition is broader and more intense. The rules and recipes for success in the legal profession have changed. To succeed today and in the foreseeable future, lawyers and law firms need to understand the practical consequences for legal services of the maturation of markets.

This chapter identifies the most influential trends shaping marketing and business development for law firms today, as well as those which are likely to continue to have a profound impact on an increasing number of legal markets worldwide. It then presents three strategic tools that any lawyer and law firm can use to win clients and add lasting value to their practice.

2. The economic challenges of a mature market

A mature market is one in which the number of lawyers seeking clients and the volume of available legal work approach equilibrium. As one after another legal market has matured since the early 1990s, the competitive forces that define successful marketing strategies for legal services have changed fundamentally.

The maturation of markets for legal services is a natural consequence of economic development and globalisation. Some of the major legal markets, such as those in North America, Europe, Australia and New Zealand, had substantially completed maturation by the end of the 1990s. Legal markets in some of the recently emerged economies, such as Brazil, Russia and Colombia, had become more or less mature by 2010. Clear signs of the market maturation process are also appearing in much of Africa and Asia, and the smaller economies of Latin America.

In short, there is more work available in mature legal markets, especially in emerging economies, but there are also more lawyers chasing it. This rough equilibrium of supply and demand typically introduces at least three difficult competitive issues for lawyers and law firms that want to build their businesses:

- Competition can create intense downward pressure on the fees that the best clients are willing to pay. Sophisticated purchasers of legal services, which previously might have been content to pay hourly rates, have started to demand alternative fee structures, such as fixed fees or success fees. This makes it imperative that law firms quote fees that are competitive in the new mature legal market, as well as profitable. Firms that have only a vague understanding of their own profitability usually get this wrong.

- Mature legal markets are frequently invaded by new non-traditional competitors, such as accountants, paralegal firms, non-lawyer trademark services and foreign law firms.
- Law firms frequently face only two options. The first is to get out of the practice area. The second option, which has longer-term promise but is more expensive and time consuming, is to re-engineer internal service delivery and administrative processes to improve high-volume productivity and reduce operational costs.
- The competition for legal talent can sometimes be even more intense than the competition for clients, particularly in markets recently entered by foreign law firms or in which companies are building large in-house law departments. It usually becomes more difficult and more expensive to recruit and retain the best young lawyers. The movement of partners and entire practice groups from one firm to another becomes a common feature of the talent market.

The consequences of market maturation can be swift and stunning. Maturation usually produces a wave of shake-outs and consolidation in the legal market. Some law firms can simply no longer compete and fail. Others abandon some traditional practice areas, in which they are no longer able to compete profitably.

Maturation also usually sets off an unprecedented number of law firm mergers and acquisitions. Small and medium-sized firms use mergers and acquisitions to consolidate stronger competitive positions, often to enhance their credibility as 'full service' firms. Foreign firms look for small or medium-sized local firms for merger, affiliation or outright acquisition, in order to establish quickly their presence as more than a representative office or sales outpost.

As a result, a common characteristic of the maturation process is that the number of law firms competing for sophisticated transactional and litigation matters from major corporate clients can condense, often in only three or four years, to a small group of top-tier firms that pull away from the competition. Such a group would now command a combined market share that could be as high as 65% to 70% in some practice areas and jurisdictions.

These factors exist to some extent in every legal market, but drive the maturing ones. They require a special focus on the development of persuasive competitive advantages that clients perceive as beneficial.

3.   New competitive advantages

It might appear that a mature legal market is driven primarily by price competition. The downward pressure on fees and the incursion of non-traditional service providers sometimes combine to spark a price war among local law firms. This can sometimes result in law firms doing legal work at a financial loss merely to retain clients and perhaps attract new ones from their traditional local competitors.

Such a race to the bottom is usually only a short-term reaction. Partners of price-cutting law firms soon become unwilling to endure low profitability without results.

The loss-leader pricing concept seldom works in a maturing legal services market. The losses continue, but rarely lead to new clients or higher-priced work.

The price warriors in a maturing legal market also soon discover that offering the lowest fees creates no more than an ephemeral competitive advantage. All that a competitor needs to do to destroy your lowest fee competitive advantage is to cut its fees to one euro, one pound, or one dollar lower than yours.

As lawyers and law firms respond to these pressures and begin to find their way in this new competitive environment, the range of fees charged by various competitors tends to compress. With most credible competitors charging more or less the same fees for the same services, clients increasingly base their selection of a lawyer on non-economic factors. Surveys conducted by Walker Clark, LLC between 2002 and 2011 of clients of law firms in mature or maturing markets clearly identify these new competitive advantages as ones that are based on client service, not price. The four most decisive factors in the selection of a law firm have consistently been:

- availability of a partner;
- responsiveness;
- understanding of the client's business; and
- the prior relationship with the firm.

Although clients always report it as important, price is never one of the top factors.

So, to build their businesses, lawyers and law firms must refocus their marketing communications and business development efforts on these new service-related indicators. More importantly, they must also be able to demonstrate how they consistently deliver service quality, rather than just talk about it in marketing brochures and on websites.

4.   Client satisfaction: good news and bad news

Another complicating factor is that as a group, law firm clients are very pleased with the services that they receive. Client surveys conducted by Walker Clark, LLC, for example, report that an average of more than 92% of all law firm clients are either "satisfied" or "very satisfied" with the overall quality of the services received. It is not unusual to see the satisfaction rate as high as 98% or 99% for some law firms.

Combined with the decisive impact of a prior professional relationship in the selection of a lawyer or law firm, high ambient levels of client satisfaction in most legal markets – even maturing ones – quickly narrow the range of opportunities for a law firm seeking new clients.

Winning a new client frequently means taking one of the very few dissatisfied ones away from a competitor. This is made even more difficult by the costs involved with switching, which clients think prevent them from firing their current law firms. They believe, with some reason, that it is better to suffer less than completely satisfactory service or disappointing results than to pay a new firm to become fully conversant with their business.

The combination of these characteristics of the mature legal market strongly point to a business-building strategy based on developing the full opportunities that might be latent in a law firm's existing client base.

5. **Beyond the myth of the 'natural rainmaker'**
    Too many lawyers believe that only 'natural rainmakers' can win new clients. This is possibly one of the biggest factors in poor marketing and business development in law firms. Not believing that they can be good at marketing, many lawyers discourage themselves and are sometimes discouraged from trying, even by colleagues and consultants.

    Successful marketing actually involves a set of skills. Some people, because of personality or personal interest, acquire these skills more quickly or feel more comfortable exercising them, but effective marketing and sales skills can be learned and mastered by anyone.

    When one strips away the academic theory and jargon from most guides to marketing and sales techniques, what remains are basic behaviours and attitudes. These competencies are useful in many aspects of everyday life and human relationships. They are especially powerful in selling legal services in a highly competitive market that might already be overcrowded with excellent lawyers and law firms. They include observable behaviours that are evidence of:

    - optimism;
    - adaptability;
    - achievement orientation;
    - empathy;
    - organisational awareness; and
    - influence.

    Learned behaviours such as these are important to building a legal practice, but many lawyers focus intently on them without also considering the overall strategic context in which those skills are to be applied. Winning clients and adding value to one's practice are more than a matter of sales skills. This is one reason why so many of the generic sales and marketing courses that lawyers take produce disappointing results. Skill without strategy is like a bow and arrow without a target.

    So can lawyers and law firms create and execute realistic strategies to win new clients and keep current ones in rapidly changing markets for legal services? Since the 1990s, three methodologies have emerged for identifying opportunities for the best possible return:

    - strong clients;
    - profitable legal work; and
    - sustainable business growth.

6. **Strategic business units: where to focus the marketing investment**
    First of all, focus.

    A first step to winning new clients and adding lasting value to a legal practice is to decide where to make the considerable investment of time, intellectual capital and resources needed to build it. With so many possibilities, what are the best targets for your firm?

    The best place to start is with your existing strengths, defined in terms of the legal specialities and practice areas that you offer and the business sectors represented by your current clients. It almost always requires less investment to build on present strengths than to attempt to establish a competitive position in an entirely new area. It is also less risky.

7. Two fascinating questions

Start with your current practice areas and service, such as litigation, corporate finance or tax. Ask these two questions:

- Which of my practice areas are currently most profitable? Focus on current practice areas, not ones that you would like to offer or that you think might be profitable. Look at each area's current profitability, not how profitable it could possibly become. Finally, focus on the word 'most'. It is possible that all of your practice areas are profitable to some extent. The purpose of this analysis is to identify those that are the most profitable.This question is not as easy as it might first appear. To answer it, some firms must scrutinise profitability by practice area for the first time. Be sure that your conclusions are supported by actual financial data, such as fee revenues, fully loaded operating costs per hour and the average profit per fee earner hour. Without data, you are only guessing.
- Which of my practice areas offer the greatest growth potential over the next five years? If you are already in the happy position of having a large share of the market for a particular service, there is probably not much growth potential. Likewise, in markets where a relatively small number of firms have a high combined market share, such as 70% or more, there is little opportunity for any one firm – even yours – to achieve significant growth, other than by merging with one of your competitors. Some of the best data on this point will usually come from your clients. Ask them about their long-term business strategies and plans. Do they foresee a significant increase in their needs for legal services? If so, what types of services will they need more in the future?

Repeat this same analysis for different industry sectors, such as banking, hospitality and telecommunications. The business-sector evaluation can produce some interesting insights by which to guide your marketing strategy. For example, you might discover that:

- some of the business sectors represented in your current client base are more profitable than others. This can also vary considerably among clients in the same sector, but in different countries; or
- growth opportunities might be short-lived. If an industry sector is entering a period of consolidation, the number of potential clients might decrease sharply, reducing the growth potential for law firms that target that industry. Instead of winning new clients, your firm probably will lose clients, as some of them go out of business due to a merger or withdrawal from the market.

8. Identifying your strategic business units

This analysis sorts the possible combinations of current profitability and growth potential into four general categories:

- high profitability/high growth potential;
- high profitability/low growth potential;
- low profitability/high growth potential; and
- low profitability/low growth potential.

When deciding on targets for marketing and business development efforts, you may disregard the last two categories.

Low profitability/low growth potential services and client sectors, frequently called the 'dogs', offer almost no potential. In fact, a law firm should consider divesting these sectors altogether. There are sometimes good reasons to keep the dogs, such as to provide a low-profit service to an otherwise profitable client; but then they should be treated as cost centres and not as targets for further investment.

Likewise, most law firms will disregard the category of low profitability/high growth potential as too speculative. Even if a practice area does offer high growth potential, its relatively low profitability will seriously reduce the return on investment. There are usually better opportunities.

Investment should instead focus on the two high-profitability categories. These are your strategic business units. They are most likely to provide stable and sustained growth for your business.

The high profitability/low growth potential category contains your firm's cash cows. Your main objective for these practice areas and business sectors should be to retain your existing clients, while looking for opportunities to introduce them to other profitable services offered by your firm. Cash cows sometimes have limited potential as referral sources for new clients, but their primary values are to build profitability and provide the financial resources to fund aggressive client development efforts in practice areas and business sectors that you have identified as having high growth potential.

The best return on investment usually comes through focusing marketing resources on the high profitability/high growth potential category. These are sometimes called the 'stars'. This does not mean that you or your firm should invest heavily in entirely new practice areas or client sectors in which you are not already present. Nor does it mean that you should disregard other reasonably profitable new clients and new instructions. However, this is where you should focus your time, attention, effort and resources.

Such an analysis can also identify very specific marketing targets, defined by business sector and practice area, that offer enormous potential. For example, if you have identified environmental regulation as a star practice area and the mining sector as a star business sector, this may suggest that your firm should make special efforts to market your environmental regulatory practice to prospective clients in the mining industry.

This analysis explains why a full service law firm marketing strategy usually produces weak results for most firms. When a law firm claims to offer full service, it often spreads its marketing efforts and resources too thinly over a broad range of potential clients and services. The better investment is to focus on those that offer the best long-term opportunities. Care for the cash cows and aim for the stars.

To summarise, the first strategic tool for winning new clients and adding value to your practice is to focus your marketing and business development efforts on your strategic business units:

- Focus marketing and business development effort on practice areas and client sectors that have high current profitability and high growth potential.
- Invest in ongoing client relations and cross-marketing of new services, primarily to keep current clients and to maintain your competitive position and profitability.
- Consider divesting from low profitability/low growth potential practice areas and business sectors to the greatest possible extent. Only continue to provide low profitability/low growth potential services to current clients which are otherwise profitable. Do not include this category in your marketing strategy as a target for any significant investment.
- Rather than investing in marketing efforts for low profitability/high growth potential clients, work instead on improving their profitability, if possible. If significant improvements are not possible, treat them as you would the dogs, by divestiture or as cost centres for business development with current clients. Do not include this category as a target for any significant marketing investment.

9. **Client base analysis: which clients have the greatest strategic value?**

The second strategic method examines the firm's existing client base. How well do you understand your current client base? Which clients offer the best opportunities for future growth? Which ones are most likely to hold you back?

There is an interesting phenomenon, known as the '80-20 rule', that may be found in the client base of most law firms. It has been observed across a wide range of practice specialties and in firms of all sizes.

Simply stated, the 80-20 rule holds that a disproportionately large share of a law firm's fee revenue is produced by a relatively small number of its clients. Although the proportions vary, actual measurements of the 80-20 rule demonstrate that in most law firms, roughly 10% to 25% of the clients, as a group, produce between 75% and 90% of the fees.

Client base analysis identifies which clients belong in which levels or tiers of the client base. The table on the following page represents the fee distribution of a general commercial practice firm with 30 lawyers.

This example is not intended to be a benchmark or best practice model. Instead, it shows how fee revenues tend to concentrate in a small portion of a law firm's total client base. The ranges for the fee levels are highly firm-specific. In a much larger firm, the threshold for the top clients might be much higher.

In this example, the top three levels of clients together constitute only 23.1% of the total number of clients, but contribute 85.3% of the fee revenue. By contrast, the small clients make up 75.9% of the total, but produce less than 6% of the fees.

The more important impact of the 80-20 rule (or in the example above, the '85-23 rule') is on profitability. As a general rule, the clients in the upper tiers of the client base not only produce a disproportionate amount of the fee revenue, but are

Level	Number of clients	Total fees produced by each level	% of all clients	% of all fees
Top clients Range: more than $1 million in fees	5	$6,800,000	3.4%	60.5%
Large clients Range: $100,000 to $1 million in fees	11	$1,600,000	7.6%	14.2%
Medium clients Range: $10,000 to $100,000 in fees	19	$1,190,000	13.1%	10.6%
Small clients: Range: under $10,000 in fees	110	$645,000	75.9%	5.7%
Totals	145	$11,235,000		

also more profitable, as a group, than those in the lower tiers. In fact, in some law firms the small clients actually produce a financial loss for the firm.

An understanding of the relative financial contribution of each level of your client base leads to some important strategies to build the value of the practice such as the following:

- Movement within the client base – be aware of the movement of clients between levels over a period of between three and five years. If a client that was in the top tier for two or three years slips down to the large-client tier, or even lower, be absolutely certain that you know why. Likewise, watch the movement of smaller clients up into higher levels of the client base. These movements, up or down, can sometimes be important indicators of significant shifts in the needs for legal services within a business sector. They can also sometimes suggest systemic client satisfaction, particularly if you observe a significant movement of more than two or three of your top clients. On the other hand, client movement within the client base might be the result of the billing cycle, particularly if your firm handled a major litigation matter for the moving client. It could also reflect a natural, but not strategically important, change in client demands for legal services. Whether migration is a significant strategic indicator or merely a benign phenomenon, you and your firm need to understand why it happens.
- Special attention to the clients in the upper levels of the client base – because top clients often are also some of a law firm's most productive cash cows,

they are good targets for cross-marketing of other profitable legal services. The top and large clients that remain in the upper levels of the client base year after year can also be a powerful marketing force for a law firm. They warrant special treatment and can be very influential in referring your firm to others in the same industry sector or in the business community.

- The strategic puzzle of the medium clients – although it is usually not worthwhile investing heavily in marketing to the lower levels of the client base, there will always be exceptions. The medium clients usually pose the most challenging strategic problems. Some may have been faithful clients for years, although not very productive ones. The growth potential of many of these long-term, mid-level clients is usually limited, and the probability of one of them referring a lucrative new client to your firm might be about the same as winning a lottery. The key strategy for adding value to the middle levels of your client base is to identify those that demonstrate clear potential for profitable legal work and work hard to get more instructions from them. In other words, promote them. In the example above there might be only one or two medium clients that offer significant business development potential, but it is important to know who they are.

- At the bottom of the client base – significant efforts in marketing and client relations among small clients, even traditionally loyal ones, seldom produce a good return on the investment and sometimes result in no return at all. However, as with the medium clients, be sure that you understand why the long-term small clients have remained small and look for any reasonable opportunity to move them up to the next level.

Understanding the relative revenue production positions of clients in your client base can also help you to identify those that you should be consulting on issues of expectations of service quality and how your firm compares to your competitors. One of the practical consequences of focusing on the top is that it simplifies client surveys and other client feedback activities. The top and large clients typically demonstrate the highest rates of responses to client surveys, are the most enthusiastic participants in client interviews and can provide valuable insights as members of client advisory boards and focus groups.

10. Competitive advantage and differentiation: why instruct our firm?

The third strategic methodology for winning clients and building value is to define and demonstrate the competitive advantages that differentiate your firm. In other words, why should a client select your firm over all of the other professionally excellent, honest, hard-working alternatives?

The first step is to develop a very clear understanding of how your clients define quality in the legal services that they receive. Even in high-volume or commodity legal work, merely meeting basic needs will seldom win a sophisticated new client. Today's sophisticated clients expect more.

Clients define quality in terms of specific service attributes, such as the availability of partners and the firm's reputation, responsiveness and understanding of the client's business. The nature and relative priority of these quality indicators often vary among business sectors and with respect to the various practice areas that a law firm offers. (This can be particularly troublesome for full service law firms that assume that all clients want more or less the same thing.)

Ask your clients these four questions and listen carefully to their answers:

- What do you consider to be the most important indicators of quality in the delivery of legal services? Persuade your clients to define quality in terms of specific, observable behaviours, not attitudes. For example, if a client says, "It is important to me that my lawyer understands my business", ask it to describe the behaviours and actions that demonstrate that a lawyer really does understand. It is observable, and sometimes even measurable, actions that distinguish true competitive advantages from marketing slogans.

- How important is each quality indicator? Of course, all of the things that the client mentions are important. However, which ones are decisive – so important that the client might base his or her choice of a lawyer or law firm on that factor alone? Conversely, the absence of a decisive factor may also be expressed as a reason to fire a lawyer.

- How frequently does your firm meet each expectation? If a client indicates that you are not meeting a decisive expectation always or almost always, this is a clear danger signal. In a mature market, the most attractive target clients for other law firms are those relative few which are dissatisfied. There is a very high risk that your dissatisfied client this year will be someone else's client next year.

- How does your firm compare to other firms that the client has used? This is the start of insight into your firm's possible competitive advantages. Do not be afraid to probe this question deeply. If the client appears to be comfortable discussing specifics, ask for illustrative examples.

There is no best practice or most reliable instrument for collecting this information. The traditional client survey offers consistency and the ability to gather a large body of information relatively quickly. Individual client interviews are more time consuming and frequently more difficult to schedule, but they can provide much more depth and detail than a survey alone. Some law firms begin with a more general written survey and follow up with individual interviews with their top clients.

Asking the questions is more important than the form or format that is used. Avoid the common misconceptions that many lawyers and law firms have about client feedback. Here are a few of the more common examples:

- We already know what our clients want – when law firm partners and their clients are given the same surveys, there is almost always a significant gap between partner assumptions and client opinions about one or more quality indicators. Sometimes the gap is positive in nature: the partners underestimate the level of satisfaction in their clients. More often, however, the partners underestimate the importance that clients ascribe to those elements by which they define quality.

- Clients do not like to participate in surveys – this is an enduring myth of client relations in the legal profession. However, the fact is that the overwhelming majority of clients are delighted to be invited to complete a survey about the quality of the services that they receive. One reason for this is that, contrary to another widely held misconception in the legal profession, the clients of law firms are not over-surveyed. Your survey or request for an interview about client service might be the first one that a significant portion of your clients has ever received.
- Clients are not candid in their answers – lack of candour can be a problem, even in written surveys. The best way to manage a possible reluctance on the part of clients to answer honestly is to have the survey conducted confidentially by a third party. Concerns that the clients will not be entirely truthful, will be reluctant to criticise or do not want to hurt feelings arise more frequently in interviews, but still relatively rarely. Sometimes this risk can be reduced by engaging a third party, such as a consultant, to conduct the interviews.

11. Differentiation: how can we stand out in the crowd?

Differentiation is the second step to building the competitive advantage needed to win new clients in a mature legal market. Being good is not enough. To build sustainable growth for a legal practice, lawyers and law firms must be able to demonstrate clear superiority over their competitors with respect to issues that are important to clients.

11.1 Why is differentiation so important?

Even excellent law firms with outstanding lawyers and great sales skills never get noticed, especially in emerging legal markets. They are virtually unknown to prospective clients and referral sources. Their website and marketing materials might actually disqualify them from serious consideration.

Any strategy to win new clients must deal with five hard truths about competition in maturing legal markets:

- Meeting the basic requirements of a prospective client does not win you the instruction. It means only that you are not disqualified from the start.
- Sophisticated clients select a lawyer or law firm based on their perceptions of the differences between the candidates. Who can meet my needs best?
- The larger the market segment in which a firm competes, such as full service corporate or litigation, the more qualified competitors.
- The greater the number of qualified competitors, the more difficult it is for one firm to stand out as clearly the best qualified.
- Finally – and most important of all – if your firm cannot explain how it is different from its competitors, do not expect the prospective client, or one of the rankings directories, to figure it out for you. Failure to differentiate is a confession that there is no compelling reason to select your firm over your competitors.

In maturing legal markets, merely being different is not the same thing as differentiation. To be effective, your firm's differentiation should satisfy the following criteria:

- Relevant to the client – don't waste time boasting about your technology or your new state-of-the-art offices. Clients expect law firms to have adequate information technology and internet-based communications systems. Talk about fancy offices and great art collections can scare clients about the fees that such a firm must charge. Instead, show how your strengths benefit the client. For example, if your firm has special knowledge and insight of an industry sector, such as oil and gas, explain how that understanding of the oil and gas client's business enables you to produce better legal results more efficiently.

- Credible – sophisticated consumers of legal services usually know when a law firm's marketing claim has no real substance to support it. For example, a 10-lawyer law firm that claims "world-class expertise" in 20 practice areas immediately invites scepticism, as well as dismissal of any claims that might be more or less true. The problem is that the claimed differentiation appears at face to be incredible, even if it has an arguable factual basis.

- Clear – a differentiating competitive advantage should include some benefit that is unique or virtually unique to your firm. With the many excellent law firms and lawyers that are competing for the best clients, it can be difficult to describe a particular feature or benefit of your service as truly unique to the legal profession. However, some well-managed firms can consistently deliver a level of quality in a particular area, such as the availability of partners, that is so far above that offered by other firms as to be nearly unique to the market.

- Provable – if you want your claim of differentiating competitive advantage to be taken seriously, you must be prepared to prove that you deliver it consistently.

- Sustainable – promising to return every client's telephone call within 90 minutes would certainly differentiate you. It would also be highly relevant, clear and provable. But for how long could your firm sustain such performance?

- Understood by everyone in the firm – in a highly competitive, mature legal market, competitive advantage is too difficult to establish to have it depend on a relatively small number of partners. For example, if you claim that your firm is one of the best in the market for dealing with the needs of foreign clients, you must be sure that everyone who answers a telephone is reasonably fluent in English. Everyone in the firm needs to understand what client-oriented behaviours are important to the firm's success and, equally importantly, why they are important.

12. Using the tools together

This chapter has introduced three simple strategic methodologies for winning clients and building sustainable business performance. Each one can lead to dramatic improvements in the marketing and business development of any lawyer and any law firm:

- The evaluation of strategic business units can help you to focus on a relatively small, manageable number of business sectors and practice areas that offer the best long-term return on investment;
- The client base analysis can help you to identify the current clients that hold the strategic keys to your firm's future; and
- Client feedback can help you to articulate compelling and differentiating reasons prospective clients should select your firm from a field of excellent competitors.

Used together, in the sequence in which they are presented in this chapter, these tools can help your firm to attract new clients which can contribute to your economic growth and market reputation, even in the most challenging of market conditions.

About the authors

Norman Clark

Managing principal, Walker Clark LLC

norman.clark@walkerclark.com

Norman Clark is one of the founders and currently managing principal of Walker Clark LLC, an international legal management consultancy based in the United States.

He advises law firms worldwide on business strategy, partnership structure and governance issues, practice management systems, career management and compensation systems. He is also one of the world's leading authorities on management and marketing for law firms in emerging economies. He has been a full-time business advisor to the legal profession for 18 years.

Mr Clark is a retired member of the Pennsylvania bar. He holds BS, JD, and LLM degrees. He is a past chair of the Law Firm Management Committee of the International Bar Association (IBA). In 2003 he was elected a fellow of the College of Law Practice Management, North America's most prestigious association of senior professionals in legal management.

Stephen RN Denyer

Global markets partner, Allen & Overy LLP

stephen.denyer@allenovery.com

Stephen Denyer is the global markets partner with Allen & Overy (A&O). He is responsible for leading and coordinating A&O's approach to markets in which it does not have an established presence, and for coordinating its relationships with associated firms and with firms in prospective new markets. He is also A&O's global representative at regulatory and professional bodies such as the IBA.

From 2007 to 2009 he was international development partner, a wide-ranging role related to the global development of the firm. From 1997 to 2007 he was regional managing partner for continental Europe. From 2003 to 2006 he was joint managing partner of A&O's Italian offices. From 1990 to 1997 he was the partner in charge of the firm's offices in Central and Eastern Europe. He headed the offices in Warsaw from 1995 to 1997 and in Frankfurt from 1998 to 2000.

Horst Ebhardt

Partner, Wolf Theiss

Horst.Ebhardt@wolftheiss.com

A partner at Wolf Theiss, Horst Ebhardt specialises in cross-border M&A in Central, Eastern & Southeastern Europe. Over the past 10 years, he has advised on some of the region's largest M&A transactions, including the €3.2 billion acquisition of BAWAG PSK by Cerberus and several acquisitions of banks by UniCredit.

Mr Ebhardt's expertise includes public and private M&A, privatisations and restructurings, and he regularly advises companies, financial institutions and private equity funds (and their portfolio companies) on corporate finance and governance. He holds law degrees from the University of Graz and the London School of Economics and Political Science, and teaches an M&A programme at the law school of the University of Vienna. Mr Ebhardt previously served as head of corporate and M&A, and firm-wide managing partner at Wolf Theiss.

Neville Eisenberg

Managing partner, Berwin Leighton Paisner LLP
neville.eisenberg@blplaw.com

Neville Eisenberg is the managing partner of City law firm Berwin Leighton Paisner. A corporate lawyer, he joined the firm in 1989, became a partner in 1995 and has been managing partner since 1999.

Born and educated in South Africa, he graduated in business and law from the University of the Witwatersrand in Johannesburg before qualifying to practise law in South Africa. He completed a master's in international business law at the London School of Economics in 1988 before re-qualifying as a solicitor.

As a corporate lawyer, he specialises in UK and international mergers and acquisitions, joint ventures, initial public offerings, privatisations and general corporate law.

A regular speaker on topics of law firm management and leadership, Mr Eisenberg has led Berwin Leighton Paisner's transformation into a leading London firm with a growing international presence.

Lord David Gold

Principal, David Gold & Associates LLP
info@davidgoldassociates.com

Lord David Gold is a legal strategist, a mediator and a Conservative working peer. He was also appointed corporate monitor of BAE Systems plc by the US Department of Justice in August 2010. He was formerly head of litigation and then senior partner at Herbert Smith LLP.

Instead of taking the lead in conducting litigation, Lord Gold offers to work alongside the client's existing solicitors to find a solution to the problem as an additional resource to the team. Lord Gold will bring an objective, commercial and fresh view to the problem, including a review of strategy.

Lord Gold has a pre-eminent reputation as litigator and is recognised as one of the country's leading litigators by all of the top legal directories. His clients have included many FTSE 100 and leading international companies, major investment banks and high-profile individuals.

Alan Hodgart

Managing director, Huron Consulting Group
ahodgart@huronconsultinggroup.com

Alan Hodgart is recognised as one of the world's leading strategic development advisers to professional services firms. For more than 20 years he has helped clients to improve and sustain their competitiveness by establishing effective strategic management and leadership processes.

He has worked with a wide range of international businesses, from small and mid-sized firms to some of the world's largest.

Mr Hodgart is particularly experienced at converting changes in strategy into steps for practical action, and in helping firms to build commitment to the necessary changes in behaviour. He has deep knowledge of competitive trends in the professional services markets and uses this to help clients reach a genuinely competitive position.

Mr Hodgart is the author of *Strategies and Practice in Law Firm Mergers*. He was awarded a Lifetime Achievement Award by the Managing Partners' Forum for his work with professional services firms.

Bryan Hughes

Chief executive, Eversheds LLP
bryanhughes@eversheds.com

Bryan Hughes is the chief executive of international law firm Eversheds.

Having advised the firm's clients on complex commercial litigation disputes for over 20 years, Mr Hughes was appointed UK managing partner in 2006 and chief executive in 2009. His leadership, operational expertise and desire to deliver client service excellence have been key to the continuing global success of the firm.

The dramatic post-recession shift in the relationship between clients and their external legal advisers has meant that in-house counsel and buyers of legal services can demand more from their lawyers in terms of value, efficiency and innovation. Recognising this trend early on, Mr Hughes has overseen the development of predictable pricing, innovative fee solutions and closer working relationships and partnerships with clients. The firm continuously improves its services around its clients' needs, adding commercial value to their businesses.

This forward-thinking approach led to Eversheds being named the *Financial Times'* Most Innovative Law Firm of 2010-11.

Charles Martin

Partner, Macfarlanes LLP
charles.martin@macfarlanes.com

Charles Martin joined Macfarlanes in 1983 and became a partner in 1990. He works principally in M&A and private equity, acting for sponsors and corporates. Much of his work is cross-border in nature.

The leading directories, including *Chambers*, rate him among the most highly recommended M&A and private equity lawyers in the United Kingdom.

Clients particulaly look to Mr Martin for strategic counsel and tactical input on a wide variety of legal matters, including M&A negotiations and litigation.

Recent highlights include advising:

- Brit Insurance NV on a recommended $1.3 billion cash offer by Apollo and CVC;
- the independent directors of TNK-BP in relation to a proposed transaction with Rosneft;
- CSN on its offer to acquire Corus for £6 billion; and
- Goldman Sachs on the €1.2 billion acquisition of and investment in ABN AMRO's UK, Netherlands and Nordic private equity portfolio.

Lynn M McGrade

Partner, Borden Ladner Gervais LLP
lmcgrade@blg.com

Lynn M McGrade is in the Toronto office of Borden Ladner Gervais LLP (BLG), practising in securities and capital markets, with a focus on investment, private, pooled, closed-end and segregated funds, structured products, investment management, adviser/dealer issues and securities law.

Ms McGrade is the Toronto regional coordinator of BLG's investment management group, chair of BLG's business development committee and a member of BLG's women's leadership development committee. She is a director of the National Society of Compliance Professionals (NSCP) and currently chairs the Canadian Committee of NSCP. She is also past chair of Committee I (Investment Companies and Mutual Funds) of the International Bar Association.

Past recognitions in *Lexpert* magazine include Top 40 Lawyer in Canada under 40 (2002); Top 15 Women Lawyers to Watch in Canada (2003); and Top 40 Corporate Lawyers to Watch (2006) in *Lexpert*®'s Guide to the 100 Most Creative Lawyers in Canada.

Robert Millard

Senior strategy manager, Linklaters LLP
robertfmillard@mac.com

Rob Millard is based in Linklaters' London office, with responsibilities worldwide. As part of the firm's strategy and business transformation team he provides business intelligence to the firm's senior leadership, helping them to make strategic decisions. Before joining Linklaters, Mr Millard was a partner for around a decade in a well-known law firm management consultancy.

His primary research interest is the evolution of law firm business models, especially in response to shifts in macroeconomics, globalisation and client demands. He is particularly interested in how this applies in emerging markets.

Mr Millard holds an MBA degree from Henley in England. He currently serves on the Law Firm Management Committee Advisory Board of the IBA, and has previously served on the committee of the Law Practice Management Section of the American Bar Association (ABA).

Philip Rodney

Chairman and partner, Burness LLP
philip.rodney@burness.co.uk

Philip Rodney has been chairman of Burness LLP since 2005.

In this role, he has been responsible for leading the strategy of Burness LLP, one of the most successful commercial law firms in the Scottish market.

He has written and broadcast on legal business, and is currently also chairman of The Glasgow School of Art.

Carole Silver

Professor of law, Indiana University Maurer School of Law
silverc@indiana.edu

Carole Silver is a professor of law at Indiana University Maurer School of Law. She teaches courses on globalisation and the legal profession, corporations, securities regulation, international securities regulation and comparative corporate governance, conflicts of law and the legal profession and ethics.

She has published more than 30 articles and book chapters analysing the global strategies of large law firms, the role of US legal education in the careers of international lawyers, and the relationships between the globalisation of legal services, regulation, legal education and law firm structure.

Professor Silver is also director of the Law School Survey of Student Engagement, which houses the largest national data set on US legal education from the perspective of students. She

also is a member of the ABA's Ethics 20/20 Commission and an affiliated scholar of the American Bar Foundation.

Corinne Staves

Senior associate, Maurice Turnor Gardner LLP
corinne.staves@mtgllp.com

Corinne Staves is a senior associate at Maurice Turnor Gardner LLP. As a member of the partnerships, LLPs and commercial trusts practice, she advises on the use of partnerships, limited partnerships and LLPs for professional practices, funds, fund managers, joint ventures and wealth planning vehicles. She has advised international professional firms on structure and governance, mergers and demergers, team and individual partner moves, LLP conversions and regulatory matters. She has also advised and lectured on the uses of partnerships and LLPs in estate and succession planning.

Ms Staves is a member of the Association of Partnership Practitioners.

James Tsolakis

Head of legal services, The Royal Bank of Scotland
James.Tsolakis@rbs.co.uk

James Tsolakis is head of legal services for corporate and institutional banking at The Royal Bank of Scotland. As such, he has a wealth of experience in both the banking and legal sectors. He is a banker to the legal profession with more than 12 years' experience in both London and New York.

In addition to his global responsibilities, Mr Tsolakis supports the legal sector across the United Kingdom. His clients include a number of the United Kingdom's top 100 law firms. He works with product specialists to provide advice and best practices to the legal profession across applicable banking and financial products. Mr Tsolakis supports his clients through his understanding of the legal market, and they value him as a strategic business partner.

Richard Turnor

Partner, Maurice Turnor Gardner LLP

richard.turnor@mtgllp.com

Richard Turnor leads the professional practices group of Maurice Turnor Gardner LLP. This group was established in 2009 by the former professional partnerships team of Allen & Overy LLP, which Mr Turnor also led.

Mr Turnor is ranked as a star individual in the non-contentious partnership table of *Chambers & Partners Legal Directory*, 2011. Mr Turnor advises professional and other partners, partnerships and LLPs on all aspects of partnership and LLP law and practice, including internal constitutional issues, governance, regulation, international structure, mergers, de-mergers and disputes.

Mr Turnor has extensive experience of advising LLP fund managers, and of using partnership and LLP structures in a range of commercial contexts, from joint ventures to capital markets structures. He is a former chairman and a member of the Association of Partnership Practitioners. He is also a non-executive director of the Royal Marsden NHS Foundation Trust.

Sean Twomey

Head of business development, Asia, Norton Rose (Asia) LLP

sean.twomey@nortonrose.com

Sean Twomey qualified as a solicitor in 1997 and went on to practise with Collins solicitors, a small and leading civil litigation practice in Hertfordshire. As a trainee and then a solicitor at this firm, he worked on a number of high-profile cases that gave him experience of dealing with the media.

Following his exposure to the press, he decided to make the transition from lawyer to PR professional in the legal sector. He joined the PR department of Denton Wilde Sapte in 1999 and subsequently joined Allen & Overy as PR manager for its banking department. After working in-house for a number of years, he moved to the PR agency Grandfield as account director. At Grandfield he worked with Norton Rose, which was a client, and in 2004 decided to join the legal practice as their head of PR. In 2010 he became head of business development, Asia, for Norton Rose (Asia) LLP. He is currently based in Singapore.

Emma-Jane Weider

Partner, Maurice Turnor Gardner LLP

emma-jane.weider@mtgllp.com

Emma-Jane Weider is a partner in the charity, not-for-profit and philanthropy practice of Maurice Turnor Gardner LLP.

She advises on a wide range of issues, including the powers, duties and liabilities of charity trustees, and investment, funding, taxation and trading issues. She has been particularly active in the past year advising major UK corporates on their relationships with affiliated charitable trusts, and their corporate social responsibility programmes. She also plays a pivotal role in the firm's pro bono legal advice programme. Ms Weider was a key contributor to the firm's response to the Giving Green Paper and has recently led a seminar with Cherie Booth QC about diversity in the professions.

In addition, Ms Weider advises on the creation, administration and taxation of trusts and other asset-holding structures, in both family and commercial contexts.

Ms Weider is a member of the Society of Trust and Estate Practitioners, the Charity Law Association and the European Association for Philanthropy and Giving.